SOMETHING
NEW

DOUBLEDAY

New York London Toronto

Sydney Auckland

SOMETHING NEW

Reflections on the Beginnings of a Marriage

AMANDA

BEESLEY

PUBLISHED BY DOUBLEDAY
a division of Random House, Inc.
1540 Broadway, New York, New York 10036

DOUBLEDAY and the portrayal of an anchor with a dolphin are
trademarks of Doubleday, a division of Random House, Inc.

Book design by Dana Leigh Treglia

Library of Congress Cataloging-in-Publication Data

Beesley, Amanda.
Something new: reflections on the beginnings of a marriage/
Amanda Beesley. — 1st ed.
p.   cm.
1. Marriage—United States. 2. Betrothal—United States.
3. Weddings—United States. 4. Beesley, Amanda. 5. Married
people—United States—Family relationships. 6. Adult children—
United States—Family relationships. I. Title.
HQ536.B425   2000
306.8'0973—dc21   99-40425
CIP

ISBN 0-385-49905-1
Copyright © 2000 by Amanda Beesley

1   3   5   7   9   10   8   6   4   2

FOR NICKY,
WITH ALL MY LOVE

Acknowledgments

This book wouldn't have left my daydreams without the amazing Esther Newberg, who, during her busy days of holding together the intellectual life of New York City, somehow managed to find this book the right home. My gorgeous and gifted editor, Amy Scheibe, helped me to uncover the truth in my story and gave me the push (and then the shove) I needed to write it. I'm also deeply grateful to Judy Daniels, Peter Gethers, the sages at Hollins University, Jack Horner, Chris Min, Bill Thomas, and all the folks at Doubleday.

A big thank-you to my dear friends (many of whom appear under pseudonyms in the book): my comrades from Mendham High, my girls from Barnard, my confidants in the city and those far flung. Without their late-night conversations, long lunches, and e-mail marathons, life would be a lot less interesting.

I was lucky to have been born into one amazing family and then married into another. Thanks to everyone on the Weinstock side—Betsy, Luke, Jake, and Leanne—for all their loyalty and kindness; and especially to Davis, who helped every step of the way. I am, of course, ever admiring of all the Beesleys: my wonderful father, John; Gordon and Jessie; and Tony and Sabina, who gave me smart advice. Because of my family's love and encouragement, I felt free to write this story as I saw it then and continue to feel it now.

My husband, Nicky, is my best friend, my nimble translator, my demanding reader, my personal trainer, my brilliant lover, my public relations manager, my shoulder to cry on, my chef, my traveling companion, and the love of my life. He was unfailingly reassuring and enthusiastic throughout the writing of this book, even while living his marriage under a microscope.

Finally, I want to thank my beautiful mother, Jill Beesley, for all she's given me, and for everything good that she is.

SOMETHING
NEW

Introduction

I went to my first wedding when I was eight years old. The groom was Ted Woodhouse, a college sophomore who, during his last years of high school, had been my favorite baby-sitter. I remember insisting that my mother let me wear a long white dress, the one I wore for First Communion, because at the time I was convinced that getting married meant that *everyone* wore a wedding gown. The ceremony took place in Ted's parents' backyard, a few doors down from our house. Halfway through the reception, all the guests gathered around Ted and his bride to watch as they cut a slice of wedding cake and placed it on a small plate. Ted fed a piece to his new wife on a silver fork. When it was her turn, the bride lay down the fork, picked up the slice with her hand, and, smiling wickedly, smashed the whole butter-cream mess into his face. I was horrified. Within a couple of years, Ted and his wife got divorced. I was always convinced it was because of the cake assault, and I promised myself that at my wedding there would be no cake-cutting ceremony at all.

I was eight years old, and already I had begun to write the rules for my dream wedding ceremony.

Ask a single, unsentimental, career-minded woman what she wants her wedding to be like, and it's unlikely she will tell you she's got more important things to think about. Instead she'll describe the antique emerald ring she wants in lieu of a traditional solitaire, or the simple, shell-colored wedding dress she saw in a magazine years ago, or the farmhouse setting where it would all take place. This doesn't mean she's desperate to get married—it doesn't even mean she necessarily wants to—it just means that she has been thinking about it in the abstract for as long as she can remember. Blame it on society, the media, fashion, whatever: some of the most untraditional women turn old-fashioned when it comes to weddings. I should know; I was one of them.

~

Nicky and I first met on the telephone. I was single, unsentimental, career-minded, and living on my own in the smallest apartment in New York City, sandwiched between an old lady who walked the hallways in her underwear and a female private eye who never seemed to work.

4

As an aspiring literary agent, part of my job was to meet aspiring book editors and try to get them to publish my authors' books. Nicholas Weinstock, an assistant editor at Random House, was on my list of people worth meeting in person. We arranged to have lunch on a snowy December day at a Thai restaurant on Fifty-sixth Street. He had been described as smart and efficient, which I took as a euphemism for nerdy and dull, so I was totally unprepared for the way he looked: tall and handsome, with curly, fair hair and a great smile. We sat down with our Pad Thai and gabbed about work for a few minutes, but the conversation quickly turned personal. By the end of our business lunch, the only business we had accomplished was to determine that we were both single and not dating anyone seriously, that he was twenty-four and I was twenty-six, that we both came from relatively normal families, and that we should see each other again—preferably not during work hours. We didn't actually go out on a date until a couple of months later, but from then on I was pretty sure that Nicky and I were in it for the long haul.

When I tell this story to other people I can't help elaborating on that first meeting to give the impression that we fell in love at first sight. It's not true. Yes, he was attractive, and for a Harvard graduate he was surprisingly intelligent, but I didn't know enough about him. After a few dates I found out that he had been working on a novel, and that he wanted to be a writer. After a few months I discovered that whenever I tried to trap him into

5

a category, from soft-shoed intellectual to guy's-guy sports fan, he'd slip out of it like Houdini. He was constantly surprising me, and finally the surprises were so good I began to fall in love with being surprised: he was a great cook, he was athletic, he didn't brag, he was nice to my friends, he had comfortable sweaters, he loved to read. These simple things shouldn't have been so startling, but I guess you never expect to find more than one or two things you want in one person, and when you do you stand a chance of falling in love. So for us it wasn't love at first sight, as much as I like to pretend it was. It was a series of surprises, a beautifully wrapped box that opened to reveal another, and then another, as we discovered we were in love.

During the first few years we dated, I was unsure of what I wanted to do with my life. I spent most of my twenties trying to figure it out. At first I thought publishing was the perfect place for me; I loved reading and talking about books, and I worked on my own writing whenever I could. As I started my life as a literary agent, I dabbled in other ideas as well: signing up for an acting class after work, reading books about cartooning, researching medical schools, whatever sounded interesting at the time. Nicky was always there as I practiced lines from a play or drew lines in a sketchbook or studied the literature from a host of different graduate schools. When I finally realized that what I loved doing the most was writing, he helped me put together my application for a writing program in Virginia that I'd heard about. I was accepted, and after I quit the agency he drove me and the moving van down south and visited me every other weekend for a year. He never teased me for changing and rechanging my mind, never discouraged me as I skidded from rehearsing Shakespeare to drawing stick figures to writing one-act plays. Three and a half years after our first date, we were married.

Soon after we got back from our honeymoon, *Self* magazine offered me a job writing a column, in the form of a monthly journal, about my first year of marriage. I accepted immediately, even though I wasn't sure that marriage was that remarkable or fascinating a step for couples anymore. I certainly didn't expect it to have the impact on my life that it had on the lives of women a generation before me, for whom it was standard practice to forgo college, quit a job, or leave a hometown to be with a new husband. My mother, for example, left her job as a stewardess just before she got married, moved to Italy with my father when he was transferred there just after, and started having babies within a year. Times have changed, I thought. Stewardesses have become flight attendants. Fawning, domesticated "ladies" are now ambitious "women." My female friends are waiting until their late twenties and early thirties to get married, by which time they have established careers and developed other interests. They believe in test-driving a marriage, so they date or live with boyfriends for years before making the big commitment. I was one of these women, and despite all I thought I knew about my relationship with the man I married, I learned within a few months that I had vastly underestimated how much marriage would change my life.

A lot of the changes have been pleasantly surprising. I hadn't expected that marriage would boost the way the world sees me; that I would appear more confident and well put together, as if I had won the dating game and taken home the grand prize. Being treated this way has been good for my self-esteem and confidence. On the other hand, my new image has been hard to live up to. Along with my glittering new ring and triumphant feelings of love, I emerged from my wedding day with a brand-new set of concerns about the nuts and bolts of our progress. I wondered how we were doing compared with my parents when they were my age. Would we ever have the money to buy our own place? Would we have the stability, emotional and logistical, to become parents? And if we did, what would happen to my career? Although I knew that my married friends shared some of these anxieties, for the most part they didn't share them with me. Conversations about marriage among the newly married seem to come in only one form: that of a placid, cheery assurance that everything is great. Even if things happen to stink.

As part of my job as a columnist, I began to ask some recently married women about their experiences, and to receive letters from many more, and I have discovered that many of us are overwhelmed not only by happiness but by accompanying doubts, loneliness, and expectations for the future. I was surprised; I thought that the expansive friendships and independent careers of modern women would have helped to cure the isolating effect that marriage may have had on housewives of forty years ago. But getting married these days brings as many major social changes as it ever has—shifts in a bride's relationship to her family, to her career, to her friends, and to her husband—that combine to leave her stranded.

Before the wedding, everyone barrages the bride-to-be with advice about makeup and table settings, budget and etiquette; but the moment she's married, the flurry of counsel stops. At her ceremony and reception, she can ask anyone for anything and receive a quick and smiley response; but once the ceremony's over, her questions go unanswered, and usually unasked. How do you share a life with someone without compromising who you are? How do you focus on yourself without being selfish? How do you honor your family's traditions and at the same time forge new ones of your own? How do you keep from feeling lost? The bride is sent off from her wedding in a hail of good wishes and birdseed—so who wants to hear, mere months after all the hullabaloo, that things are anything short of what she had hoped? Marriages, like lives, are made up of imperfections and disappointments as well as great romance and joy; however, most new brides are expected to talk and hear about only the good stuff.

I had begun to think that communications with my

own family would remain as solidly close (or distant) as they had always been, and that they would stay that way for the rest of our lives. In becoming a wife and still remaining a daughter, my relationship with my parents has become more loving and more complicated than I could have imagined. In some ways I have become more like them: a full-fledged adult with household concerns, oddball habits, and a spouse in the next room. In others, I am still girlishly fighting to be as different from them as possible. In every way, I am more involved with them than ever. In fact, one of the greatest challenges of my new life as a wife has been coming to terms with the one wife I've known since the day I was born.

The very same week that I got engaged, my mother was officially diagnosed with dementia, a general term for a type of neurological disease of which Alzheimer's is the most common category. This is how I have to think of the disease: in clinical, unemotional terms. How I think of my mother herself changes dramatically day to day, as I try to reconcile the painful loss of a parent with the sweet discovery of married love. "Loss" may sound like a strong word to describe a relationship with someone who's still alive, but that's the nature of this illness; I've lost my old mother, the wise and gentle woman who taught me how to swim and ski and fix a leaky faucet. Over the years she has gradually become more and more dependent on my father to help her with the simple, daily activities most people take for granted, like cooking and dressing and telling stories. Just as I was beginning to collect my own memories, of our wedding and of starting a new life with the man I loved, my mother's memories were being torn up and thrown into the wind. And as much as I wanted to collect the pieces and paste them together again, I found that I was too late. Her world was becoming trapped in the present tense at the same time as mine was opening into the future; and what I'm beginning to understand is that there isn't a simple way of bundling up all the feelings that come with that shift.

My story of becoming a wife is the story of every daughter who feels the loss, the joy, and the responsibility that comes with leaving her old family to start a new one, and of every bride who must decide, gradually or suddenly, to become her own female role model. It's not a decision that's always ours to make; many women have already lost their mothers by the time they marry. I was one of the fortunate ones: ever since the plans for my own wedding began at the age of eight, my mother was part of the daydream. I know how lucky I am to have had her with me as I walked down the aisle and into married life, and I often think about how difficult it would have been—and, at times, how difficult it is—to do it without her.

~

This book is a journal of the beginnings of a marriage, *my* marriage, and the unspoken hopes and heartaches that have come with it. Starting with getting engaged and continuing through the first year of being married, the process has been a roller-coaster, what with starting my career as a writer, then moving to the country after twelve years of city life, moving into coupledom after twenty-nine years of single life—and redefining my relationship with the one woman and wife I've known the longest.

Throughout the eight months of my engagement, as I pored over silly books about perfect weddings (as if we need advice like "Don't get drunk at your wedding," and "Remember not to complain about your in-laws in front of strangers"), I kept hoping I would find something honest about the way it feels to get married, and what it means to women these days—something more relevant and powerful than tips on cake decoration and advice on dry-cleaning old lace. Of course, no one's experiences can be absolutely universal, but I think every bride learns the same four secrets of being a wife that I did—and learns, at last, the real meaning of that strange old rhyme. Something old was my former life, instantly and awkwardly out of date. My newlywed life felt somewhat borrowed. There were still times when I felt blue.

And marriage, to my surprise, is definitely something new.

PART
ONE

The Engagement

For unmarried people in love and still on speaking terms with their families, holidays bring on difficult choices. The boyfriend and girlfriend want to be with each other, but both sets of parents want their still-single children home for one of the last family dinners before they go off and start building families of their own. After all, the empty-nested parents hint, it's *their* celebration too; and without their grown-up babies to share it with them, the holiday couldn't possibly be the same. Everyone can be flexible some of the time: Thanksgiving, for example, is always negotiable; birthdays can be celebrated a week late; anniversaries are important only every ten years or so. But the big holidays are always trouble. Unless the in-laws-to-be are living down the street from each other, someone is going to wind up compromising. And it always seemed to be us.

Although we'd been together for almost three years and living together for one, Nicky and I were planning, as usual, to spend the holidays with our respective families. After two years of missing each other as we unwrapped presents on Christmas Day, we decided to break with tradition and have our own celebration a few days early. We purchased a Christmas shrub from the guy selling trees on Second Avenue, dragged it up four flights to our little apartment on the Lower East Side, strung it with lights and goofy ornaments from Chinatown, and made a date to exchange gifts on Friday night, the day before we were leaving town to go to my parents' house in New Hampshire—and three days before Nicky would fly back to New York for Christmas with his folks.

At the time I was working as a legal secretary. After getting back from writing school in Virginia, I'd decided not to return to my day job in publishing so that I could work at night instead, the idea being that this brainless job would leave time in the mornings to write the one-act play that was going to launch my brilliant career as a brilliant writer. It seemed like a good idea at first, but after a few weeks the precious mornings dissolved back into sleep, and by the time I was up and dressed I had only an hour for myself before I had to go to the law firm again. The work wasn't easy, either. I resented making photocopies and chipper small talk for the lawyers, and I wasn't making headway as a writer during my free time. I was miserably aware that something in my life needed to change. Maybe that's why, over the previous months, I had become increasingly fixated on the idea of getting engaged. I didn't think it would suddenly make a difference in my writing career, nor did I want or expect Nicky to start taking care of me financially. But at least getting married would show initiative and progress in an otherwise stagnant life. I began to pepper Nicky with stinging hints about wanting our relationship to "move on" and veiled threats about what might happen if it didn't. We had been together for three years, and I was turning thirty in ten short months. People were beginning to ask me when I was going to get married, and instead of telling them to mind their own business, I had started to wonder myself.

When the Friday of our pre-Christmas festivities came around, I had had a typical night on the job. My assignments included running downstairs to pick up a law partner's dinner; typing a term paper for another attorney's coed girlfriend; and, for the last two hours, sitting bleary-eyed in front of the computer while a visiting lawyer painstakingly dictated an endless list of names for me to print as labels and stick onto file folders. It was clerical hell, but all was forgotten as soon as I arrived home. Nicky had arranged a spread of all my favorite pastries from De Robertis Pasticceria on First Avenue, set out biscuits for our puppy, Emma, on a separate plate, and chilled a bottle of champagne in an ice-filled plastic tool bucket.

We sat on the floor by the winking shrub, drinking bubbly, eating cannoli, and listening to the Elvis Christmas album. It was exactly the way we would have done Christmas five days later if we had both happened to be orphans. I gave Nicky his gift, an antique dress sword from the Civil War, a symbol that he, a writer as well, would always have backup for his mighty pen when times got rough. He loved the present and was genuinely moved by it—suddenly we were both on the verge of tears—but there was a gravity in the air that had nothing to do with my sentimental Christmas card. Out of nowhere we were acting strangely formal with each other, and although I wasn't thinking about getting engaged that night, I have to admit I wasn't *not* thinking about it either. Nicky handed me a large, fraying, water-stained cardboard box, tied with a ribbon. This turned out to hold a smaller package, which I unwrapped to reveal a beautiful antique silver jewelry case. This, I assumed with a mixture of disappointment and relief, was my Christmas present. Good, I thought. Everything stays the same. And then: Damn. Everything stays the same.

It would not be the first time I thought that Nicky was about to propose to me. Right before I left New York for my yearlong stint in graduate school, he took me to a fancy restaurant in Brooklyn and insisted that we be seated by the window so that we had a magical view of the Manhattan skyline. It was a perfect setup for a marriage proposal: candlelight, champagne, and a "ladies' menu" with no prices on it. My impending departure had me feeling that anything could happen, and I began to imagine that there were plans afoot. I thought I saw the waiter give us a knowing look. Nicky seemed slightly nervous. We had drinks and small talk, appetizers and dreamy looks, main courses with hands held under the table. As the meal went on, and Nicky started to seem a little more relaxed, I realized I might be on the wrong track. Finally, halfway through dessert, I blurted out, "So you're not going to propose to me, right? So I can just calm down?" Nicky was stunned. It hadn't even occurred to him. I felt like a jerk.

The next false alarm came four months later. We were in New York, exchanging presents a few days after visiting our families for Christmas. Nicky gave me a stocking full of goofy little presents: a magnetic poetry set for the fridge, a baseball cap with "Knucklehead" stitched across the front, bubble bath from the Body Shop, a candy bar—and then, at the toe, I found the tiny square box. I began to get a sick, dizzy feeling as I unwrapped it, sure that this time I couldn't be mistaken. Nicky wouldn't tease me with a *ring box*, I thought. Wrong again: inside was a pair of earrings I'd admired in a store a few weeks before.

It didn't make sense. For the first time in my life I was eager to get engaged—not just open to it, but actively enthusiastic about it—and I had the nagging suspicion Nicky was not. He'd told me that he wanted us to spend the rest of our lives together, so what was he waiting for? I was frustrated with him for dragging his feet, and annoyed at myself for acting like such a typical girl. The truth was that we were deadlocked. I saw our potential engagement as a huge, wonderful step toward our future together. My life was so unsettled in so many ways; getting engaged would settle at least one thing, maybe the most important thing of all. He, meanwhile, seemed to think that we had to build and solidify that future before topping it off with an engagement.

But back to our living room and the antique jewelry case. There I was, saying how much I liked it, trying not to sound disappointed, looking it over. Then I opened the lid (sweeping orchestral music, please) and saw the one piece of jewelry it contained: a diamond ring. Nicky dropped to one knee and asked me to marry him. Tearfully I whispered, "Yes!" We kissed, we hugged, we cried; and then I asked Nicky—because anything could happen that night—"Does this mean I get to quit my job?"

I knew the answer was no, although I was only half kidding when I asked. My sparkling career path looked more like a dismal cul-de-sac: I had a master's degree in creative writing, debt from my student loan, and the very shaky beginnings of a new career. The law firm job was not working out and I had a long way to go to become a writer. Part of me secretly hoped that marriage would somehow clear up all those problems and make us as happy for the rest of our lives as I felt at that moment. I knew it couldn't, just as I knew, every time I sent in the entry form, that I wouldn't win the Publishers Clearing House Sweepstakes; but somewhere I was hoping, just a little, for love to miraculously make everything better.

Standing next to a dwarfed Christmas tree with a diamond ring on my finger, I felt sure that my life was about to change, and wondered who I could call and tell this to in the middle of the night. After three years of being separated during the holidays, Nicky and I could finally vow that this would be the last Christmas we'd ever spend apart.

As scheduled, after the glittering Night of Cannoli, I went to spend Christmas with my folks, recently relocated from New Jersey to New Hampshire. A couple days after the excitement over my engagement settled down, my father took me aside and told me to read the letter which he'd left on my bed. It was from my mother's doctor, addressed to her, cheerily going over the results of her recent checkup. And then, with a wallop, came the only sentence I still remember: "As discussed, we have concluded that you have some form of dementia."

From the balcony upstairs I could hear my father in the kitchen, taking requests for the first round of cocktails. Directly below me, my mother was moving around the dinner table with a broom, sweeping together little piles of dust on the floor. Then, hesitating for a moment, she put the broom in the coat closet, leaving the dustpan in the middle of the table. I watched as she picked up a paper napkin, ripped it into smaller pieces, and stuffed them in her pocket. It was clear that there was no intention behind anything she did, or if she started with one, it disappeared before she could act on it. I stepped back from the railing so she wouldn't look up and see what must have been written all over my face at that moment—horror, sadness, disgust, pity, and love.

Right then I wanted Nicky, who was already back with his family in New York. I sat on my bed in a daze, trying to cry and then trying not to. My brother Tony eventually found me upstairs and suggested we go for a drive. He had read the letter the day before and felt, as I did, that it marked a turning point. We had never talked so honestly about her illness before, maybe because we had always hoped that avoiding the discussion would make it less real. It felt like a scene straight out of a miniseries on the Lifetime channel: *A family struggles with a terminal illness and discovers a new closeness and ability to love.* Except we skipped the part where we all sob together, and with insistently smiling faces went on with the holiday as if everything were fine. Such reticence is typical for my family— both my parents are British and do not believe in talking about problems. Once, in her healthier days, my mother went to a career counselor and complained afterward, "She never told me *anything*! She just kept asking me to talk about *myself*."

The revelation in the doctor's letter was a shock, but it

wasn't exactly news. My family had known things weren't fine for a long time. My mother had begun to forget things. Not the usual details we all forget, like where she left the car keys, but more telling ones, like how to balance a checkbook, or the right way to address a letter. Gradually these turned into more blatant omissions: not knowing whether she'd eaten lunch, or forgetting to take off her jacket once indoors. In a way it was a relief to finally have a doctor attempt, however lamely, to name the subtle and creeping changes we had begun to notice in her over the past five years. (The diagnosis of "dementia" is another word for ignorance—the doctors don't have the slightest idea what to do about it. Dementia is not a disease in itself but a group of symptoms, so the experts can do nothing except prescribe a few pills to allay some of the symptoms, run a few tests, and send the patient home until she gets worse.) Before this letter came in the mail, my family, along with several doctors, could only guess what the causes for her memory lapses might be: menopause, a recent move to a new town, depression, the lifestyle shift that came with my father's retirement. At least now we knew that we could give up trying to *fix* her—as if encouraging her to volunteer at the library or taking her to the Grand Canyon might reverse the damage spreading through her brain. An avid skier, cyclist, hiker, and swimmer, my mother was in great physical shape. And she was only fifty-nine years old. We never guessed that it could be anything like Alzheimer's. Or, more accurately, we were afraid to guess it.

The first real sign that something was wrong had come four years earlier. My parents had recently moved to New Hampshire, and my mother didn't seem to be adjusting very well. Although she was very involved in the community when we lived in New Jersey, she showed little interest in becoming active in her new town. I thought she might be depressed—I had read that a symptom of depression is memory loss—and I thought maybe a little time away would be good for her. I invited her to drive down and spend the weekend with me in New York City, and she took me up on the offer. Now that I look back, I wonder if she was hesitant about it, whether she knew even then that she wasn't up to the trip. The drive down usually takes about six hours. She left at ten-thirty that morning, and by five, she hadn't shown up. I called my father to see if he had heard from her, but he had not. At five-thirty she called to say that her handbag had been stolen at a gas station, but that she was fine and would be arriving in a couple of hours. At eight-thirty that night, when she still hadn't shown up, I called the state police and tried to find out if there had been any accidents on the highway. The switchboard operator had nothing to report. When I called my father, he picked up the phone before it had finished the first ring. I realized then how much he loved her, how scared he was. How serious this all was. She was driving in the dark in New York without any money, and we had no way of reaching her.

Mom finally showed up at nine-forty, five hours late. She put on a happy face, but she was exhausted. She was vague about what had delayed her, unclear about the details of the stolen handbag. It had been the worst five hours of my life; and yet, astonishing as it seems now, I pulled myself together and pretended that everything was fine. Mom and I went for walks in Central Park, had ice cream in the Village, and went shopping for a new handbag. She made it back to New Hampshire without incident.

Clearly, my mother was not the only one in denial. It took four more years and a doctor's letter to make us face the truth.

In my dictionary from college, the definition for dementia is "madness, insanity." In my own understanding it meant that my mother was disappearing, slowly and quickly, like an escaped kite against a pale sky. I was in love with Nicky and about to build a whole new life with him, and in the meantime my old life was falling apart. In that absurd way the gods have of handing out tragedies and favors, it was a time when I should have been the saddest and the happiest I had ever been. And I was.

JANUARY

Got back to New York last night, after Christmas in New Hampshire and then meeting up with Nicky for a friend's splashy, weekend-long New Year's Eve wedding. I'm already obsessing over what *not* to do for our wedding. Do not have four hundred guests in a big convention center. Do not allow the wedding singers to perform covers of songs from *Cats* and *Les Mis*. Do not choose as our wedding song the theme from Barbra Streisand's movie *The Mirror Has Two Faces*.

Almost as soon as we got on the highway heading home, a state police officer pulled us over, swaggered over to the car, and asked if we were aware that we were going fifteen miles per hour over the legal speed limit. Emma was wagging her tail and jumping all over us, unaware that she was supposed to be acting cool. The cop went back to his cruiser with Nicky's license and registration and did whatever it is these guys do for three hours, and when he came back he announced that because he had run out of tickets in his book, and because we had a cute dog, he was issuing a warning instead. I leaned over Nicky and told the cop that if he needed another reason to be nice to us, it was that we had just gotten engaged. The cop was unimpressed, as might be expected, but I couldn't help myself. I've been showing off my engagement ring to anyone who will look.

Over Christmas it turned into a family joke: Amanda allowing her left hand to linger on the salt shaker; Amanda pensively tapping her chin with her fourth finger; Amanda polishing the stone with her napkin for the twentieth time during the meal. I am full of a happy sense that everything good that happens these days, from ducking a speeding ticket to avoiding traffic on the George Washington Bridge, is a direct result of our being in love.

Nicky was sporting an old beige sweater and his unhip glasses (used only for driving and movies, and always removed immediately upon getting out of the car or theater), and behind the wheel of our shiny, rented four-door sedan, he looked adorably middle-aged and husbandish. All of a sudden, I became aware of how quickly things were changing: we were no longer a boyfriend and girlfriend on an aimless road trip, we were a real couple, grown-ups now, and we were heading home. Nicky must have been thinking the same thing, because later, as I stared out the window, thinking about that doctor's letter and what it meant for Mom and for the family, he put his hand on mine and said, "Don't get too far ahead of yourself, OK? We're going to deal with this together."

~

I love how normal, how universal, all of this feels. Everyone has something to say about getting married. Today when I was heading home after walking Emma, I ran into Stella, our neighbor from across the hall. We stood outside the building, chatting about our respective holidays, and when I told her that Nicky and I had gotten engaged, she was almost as excited as I'd been when I first put on my ring. A few hours later she showed up at my place to drop off a pile of beautiful Italian bridal magazines that she had been saving, and then we went to her place to look at her wedding album. At work, when I told one of the other secretaries my news, she launched into a description of her marriage at twenty-two, her divorce at thirty-five, and her remarriage to the same guy at forty. Everywhere I go, people want to talk about marriage.

We have set a tentative date for September 6. How weird for us to be in charge of picking a date out of thin air—it seems more like something you'd get in the mail along with your tax forms, or a notification for jury duty. So official, and so random.

~

This morning I slept in, exhausted, and when I woke up Nicky was already at his desk writing. Every morning he does the same thing: wakes up at six, does sit-ups and push-ups, makes coffee and eats a breakfast bar, and is at the computer by seven to begin work. A few weeks ago he gave his publisher the edited manuscript of his first nonfiction book, and now he's working on his first novel. In between he has published articles in all kinds of magazines. I find this both encouraging and profoundly irritating. Encouraging because this machine gunner's ambition is the sign of the kind of man who wants to provide for his family, and irritating because I've just begun in earnest *my* career as a writer, and *I* want to provide as well. I guess I'm envious of his success, and in my envy I seem to find the excuse I need to stop trying.

I have six hours ahead of me before I have to get ready for my stupid job, and I should be using the time productively, but I'm having trouble focusing. The wedding offers a too-convenient distraction. Do I start another short story that will never get published, or spend an hour with the Italian bridal magazines, trying to find the perfect dress? Do I send my play to another competition it will not win, or call other engaged friends (there are at least five to choose from) and compare notes on honeymoon destinations? I wonder if I'm going to end up planning this whole wedding by the sheer force of my ability to procrastinate. I'll plan in order to avoid working, and Nicky will work in order to avoid planning. And two months after the wedding, I will be a resentful Stepford Wife, and Nicky will be selling his damn novel to the movies.

What *is* it about Nicky that allows him to sit at his desk and work while we have only 246 days left to figure out our wedding, the Most Important Day of Our Lives?

This is where our views diverge. Nicky's reaction to our upcoming wedding is to put his head down and get work done now, whereas mine is to start planning and leave work for idle times. He's set about fixing the wobbly table that will someday hold the wedding cake, and meanwhile I'm hankering for the first bite.

Now that I've exhausted every other thought in my head, I'm left with nothing but this news about Mom. While we were in New Hampshire, the whole family went to a midnight Christmas Eve service at my parents' church. Listening to the familiar prayers, and singing carols and hymns that I've known since I was a child, I felt lost and alone. I started to cry about my mother during the Prayers of the People and didn't stop until the last chorus of "Silent Night" at the end of the candlelit service. It doesn't make sense that this should happen to someone like her, someone so sweet and good. I felt sorry for my father and for my brothers and most of all for myself. I'm not religious these days—I hung up my altar-girl robe when I was fourteen—but I prayed as hard as I could for all of us. I love her, and I don't want her to go away. I don't want her to die. I'm not ready yet. I know, I know: she's not going to die today or tomorrow; but still, a part of her is undeniably dying, whether or not she lives in her body for the next twenty years.

I've got an hour and a half until Lawyerama. I'm going to start a new short story if it kills me.

~

I'm sick, lounging around the house with a 102-degree fever. I can tell Nicky feels a new sense of responsibility for me, because he has been treating me like a baby. I have capitalized on this, to the point of asking him to carry me from room to room. We'll see how long it lasts. I look at him differently, too, now that we're pre-husband and pre-wife. I'm more relaxed about needing him now that we're officially in need of each other for the rest of our lives. I am noticing little things about him that I think are cute, like how he whistles extra-fast condensed versions of any music that happens to float by—from a TV commercial to the ice cream truck jingle—without realizing he's doing it. I wonder if this is one of those things that's going to drive me crazy when we're old.

Saw Nicky's family last night; they are so excited about the engagement. Nicky's mom, Betsy, is going to be the ringleader of this circus, I can tell. She has already bought a special notebook and begun to gather information—not to mention that she literally wrote the book on planning a wedding. (Betsy was the writer of, among many other things, Martha Stewart's book *Weddings*.) I know that traditionally, the bride's parents—and really the bride's mother—are supposed to plan and host their daughter's wedding, but my mother is in no shape to take on the job. Nicky and I talked about doing it ourselves, but as soon as we realized that Betsy was willing to take the helm, we were relieved. I suppose we're lucky in that we won't have to worry about an epic power struggle between our mothers. Or is that just another wedding myth? I think the old Jill Beesley would have been jealous if she knew how much time I'm spending with my future mother-in-law these days, clipping pictures of dresses from bridal magazines and beginning to plan the reception. Sometimes I feel like a traitor. How can I be so guilty and so giddy at the same time?

~

Last night I dreamed there were three boa constrictors chasing me: one golden, one black, and one brown. As I ran I could hear them hissing in my ear. OK, Freud fans, let me take a shot at this one. The golden snake chasing me is the wedding, coming up on me whether I'm ready or not. The black snake is dementia, coming for my mother and for me. And the brown . . . I'm not sure about the brown. Maybe the shit I've been writing lately.

I am scared to death of losing my mind when I'm fifty-five. I picture Nicky feeding me baby food and changing my diapers. I wish those scientists out there would get moving on figuring out how to cure this thing. Not that I have made a serious effort to learn about what dementia really is—I think I'm afraid of more bad news. Sometimes I catalog all the amazing things that my mother has taught or passed on to me: an immediate and usually dead-on feeling about whether people are mostly good or mostly evil; love of all birds, except crows and pigeons; a great recipe for English trifle; an understanding of the importance of looking beautiful for one's beloved, especially during a fight or when asking a favor; and a set of good teeth (definitely not from my father's side of the family). As much as I appreciate these gifts, I'd trade them all to avoid receiving the one inherited trait I fear—for the chance to be one of those spunky old ladies who remembers what she had for lunch a half-century ago. Part of this comes from the fact that I haven't been overwhelmingly successful as a young person. I never won any big awards in high school, my performance in college was average, and I didn't have the foggiest notion of what I wanted to *do* with my life until just last year. I've always planned to have my fifties be my most successful decade. I'm so scared my golden years are going to be as black as the snake from my dream.

My most unequivocal triumph to date has been meeting and getting engaged to Nicky. Here is a place where I have excelled in my field. I have fallen in love and had that love returned by a smart, funny, handsome man—a *good man*, as my friend Karen calls him. When I was twenty, I would have expected that something more impressive than falling in love would be my greatest success in the seven years after graduating from college, but now I can't think of anything that would beat it. I know it must sound pathetic, but it's not. This feeling of accomplishment has set me up to expect and strive for new successes, big or small.

~

OK, my engagement ring hurts. Literally. I think there's something wrong with the setting. The diamond—my supposed best friend—is poking my finger, which is starting to irritate my skin. I haven't told Nicky yet. I don't want to have a problem with my ring. I'm supposed to love my ring. Then again I know very few women who actually, honestly loved their rings when they got them, except for the ones who steered their fiancés to the store and told them exactly which one to buy. This is something nobody tells you about being engaged: your ring, gorgeous and precious as it may be, just might bug the hell out of you.

It's not just the accessories, either. I've noticed that people don't always react ideally when I tell them I'm getting married; maybe Nicky and I are past the blissful stage where snide remarks went unnoticed. For example, my friend Abby responded by moaning that *she* had been thinking about getting married that same weekend—now she wouldn't be able to reschedule the date for another six months. It was a silly thing for her to say, but I couldn't help feeling hurt that she wasn't happier for me. Far worse was my recent conversation with Jared. When I told him the news, he launched into a diatribe about how everyone he knows is "panicking" and "desperate to get married before they turn thirty." He assured me that he loved being single and planned to stay that way for a long time. I was so surprised by the violence of his reaction that I didn't know how to respond. Jared is one of those guys who plays in a band, writes for an alternative newspaper, and is dating a different girl every time I talk to him. As I talked about my wedding plans, I felt dull and conventional, as if marriage were some stodgy idea that went out of style with Dorothy Hamill haircuts. It never used to be this way between us: my friendship with Jared has always made me feel as if we were kindred souls, despite the fact that I don't take off every couple of months to play the bongos in Hawaii. Now all of a sudden I was letting him down. I had turned into one of "them."

I know I took both of these conversations way too seriously. These days I'm ultrasensitive to anything that sounds like less than total enthusiasm for me and Nicky, knowing that under the pretty, reflecting surface of this engagement is the murky but indisputable fact that marriage is not easy. If it were easy, half of the people who got into it wouldn't get divorced. But I refuse to dwell on how hard it's going to be. Until September 6, my marriage is perfect, because until then, it exists only in my imagination. The engagement, however, is already a reality, and a mere three weeks after the fact, life is back to its old tricks. My ring hurts. Friends don't always say exactly what you want to hear. Working for lawyers sucks. Call it the afterbuzz: one minute I'm on top of the world and the next I'm letting a bongo-playing Deadhead get under my skin.

~

We had dinner last night with the newly married Tara and David, who went glowingly on and on about how our wedding is going to be exactly like theirs: how I'm going to cry when I walk down the aisle (so says Tara), and Nicky's going to wish he were still at the wedding having fun rather than in a hotel room with me (according to David). As if theirs is the only experience that we could possibly have. When they weren't boring us with these irrelevant and depressing details, they seemed to be fighting a lot. I understand the urge to pass on some of the information that's amassed prewedding (and rendered instantly useless postwedding), but it's annoying when people talk as if your life is going to turn out exactly like theirs or else fall short. Especially when they've only been married for a year.

True, most wedding ceremonies go basically the same way: service, cocktails, dinner, band . . . but a marriage has to have a few more options. I want to feel that Nicky and I are special—the most extraordinary couple ever to come together—and I don't want to hear that we're going to get in tiffs over housecleaning or money or whose turn it is to pick up the laundry.

Now I've said that, I'm sure it's going to happen. Damn those people.

36

~

I have now done my first round of serious wedding dress shopping. A few days ago, my friend Sonya and I went to the most upscale bridal shop we could think of. I always used to think that I would get married wearing something stridently unbridal, like a simple sundress or a cool tuxedo, but what my married friends say is true: one day of trying on princessy white dresses, and there's no turning back. The same thing happened to me the first time I tried on an "interview suit" at Macy's after I graduated from college: as I stood there, admiring myself in a cream silk shell and a black blazer and skirt, I was dazzled by how respectable I looked. I would've filled out an application for law school then and there, just to be assured that someday I would wear a black suit as part of my job.

The Vera Wang boutique on Madison Avenue is a ca-thedral devoted to the silent worship of all things bridal. The women who work there are thin, pursed, and unsmil-ing, as if overwhelmed by the responsibility at hand. Sonya and I checked in at the front desk, then climbed a wide spiral staircase and took a seat in an open room with taste-fully decorated chairs on one side and a wall of mirrors on the other. A saleslady introduced herself to us, asked me what my budget was, and offered us some tea. I told her—just for the hell of it—that price was no object. She left for a few minutes and came back with an armful of dresses, showing me into a private dressing room that was about

37

the same size as my apartment. On the wall hung several silk bustiers to choose from, as well as a pair of white shoes in exactly my size. The very first dress I tried on fit perfectly. I swept out of the dressing room in this stunning strapless gown that screamed major motion picture, took my place in front of the long mirror, and looked around. Seven years after that interview suit changed the way I looked at myself, I was modeling my first real wedding dress, and suddenly all I wanted to be was a movie star bride. However, it turned out I wasn't the only wannabe trying out for the role.

The world of wedding dress shopping is a lot like high school: there's always going to be one girl who's the most popular. As it happened, this was my lucky day. To my left, modeling an ill-fitting Scarlett O'Hara hoop dress, was a slightly overweight girl with thick, dark glasses. To my right, in a bulging shift, was a pimply woman with overbearing parents. As I spun around in front of Sonya, I was Cinderella for fifteen minutes. The parents to my right turned away from their daughter and told me that I looked beautiful. My ugly stepsisters seethed. When I asked how much the dress was, the saleslady told me $9000. She added that this price did not include roughly $500 for alterations. I told her as casually as I could that I needed to think about it.

I thought about it the whole next day as I rode the subway to the infamous Kleinfelds in Brooklyn, a megastore that offers, as they say, a "wider range" of prices. I walked through the doors into a maelstrom of mothers and daughters arguing, bored men drinking Styrofoam cups of coffee, and frantic salespeople screaming last names into a microphone. Things got off on the wrong foot with Marta, my designated saleslady, when I stripped down to my underwear and she beheld my dirty sweat socks, my grandmotherly underpants, and, worst of all, my only strapless bra: a black spandex tube top. "What is *that*?" she asked, pointing at my chest. "You're not doing yourself any favors with that thing, you know. Your boobs are okay, but you're smashing them in. The idea, in case you haven't heard, is to *lift* and *separate*. See?" She demonstrated impatiently, cupping her hands and pushing her own breasts out and up.

Chastened, I crammed myself into the ivory gown she'd handed me. It had a modified halter top which, flattened boobs notwithstanding, made me look like a linebacker. As I squinted and tilted my head, trying to picture what I'd look like if the dress actually fit me, imagining away the fluorescent lights and my double chin, a new Cinderella emerged from her dressing room. Marta the Traitor dropped her pins in breathless enthusiasm as this girl twirled and giggled in her perfect white dress, knowing—perhaps for only the second time in her life—that she'd found the One.

The other thing I kept thinking as I stood there alone

in a gaudy puff of tulle, twenty-nine years old and totally independent, was that I wanted my mother. Knowing that she would never again be able to drive down and spend a weekend with me made me miss her terribly. After all, isn't looking for a wedding dress the ultimate mother-daughter project? How come all the other girls in the dress shop had their mothers by their sides?

It's easy to blame this on the fact that she's not all there these days, but the truth is, even before she started to become disoriented, before this disease kicked in for real, Mom wouldn't have fallen over herself to schlep around the city in search of the wedding dress of my dreams. She wasn't the type. On typical summer weekends, while most ladies in town played doubles tennis, catered their children's baseball games, or shopped for cotton sweaters at Talbot's, my mother took rock-climbing classes, went bird-watching, and occasionally browsed for bargains at the local army-navy store. One spring, while we were still in school, my parents left us with a baby-sitter and spent a long weekend hiking and camping on the Appalachian Trail. When they returned, lean and tanned, smelling of bug spray, I was proud of how cool they were. But even then, I could tell that this picture would never include me. I was a product of the suburbs: I liked *General Hospital*, hanging out at the Rockaway mall, and driving around town with my girlfriends. My idea of the great outdoors was lying out in the backyard, slathered with baby oil, trying in vain to get my white English skin to turn dark brown.

So we have our differences, my mother and I. And planning this wedding brings up the hidden, shameful part of me that wants the other kind of mother: the kind who takes her daughter to a spa for a weekend, who hands out hints on keeping thin and tweezing eyebrows, who looks at your outfit and says, "You're not going out of the house like *that?*" The kind of mother who cries when she sees her daughter in a wedding dress for the first time. It's an idealized picture, I know. It's easy to observe mothers and daughters from the outside and imagine their perfect friendship. I don't know what it would have been like to plan a wedding with my mother, the "other mother" with whom I grew up. Maybe Mom and I would have had a great time together looking at dresses. Or maybe we would have quibbled over money and argued about the guest list. It could have been a nightmare, for all I know. But it would have been fun to try.

I keep wondering what it was like for my mom when she got engaged: what advice she got from her mother, how my father proposed, how she felt in the months leading up to her wedding day. But she can't remember any of it. My father can fill in some of the blanks, but it's not the same. How do I answer all my questions about being a wife without the help of the wife I know best?

~

Lately I'm rereading any books that I can think of that are about marriage: *Madame Bovary*, *The House of Mirth*, *Sense and Sensibility*. Of course, with the exception of the Austen, they all end in despair, but halfway through *Anna Karenina*, I found the perfect description of what it feels like to be engaged. In this passage Kitty is about to get married and is looking back at the past six weeks since becoming engaged to Levin:

> . . . There took place in her heart a complete severance from all her old life, and a quite different, new, utterly strange life had begun for her, while the old life was actually going on as before. Those six weeks had for her been a time of the utmost bliss and the utmost misery. All her life, all her desires and hopes were concentrated on this one man, still uncomprehended by her, to whom she was bound by a feeling of alternate attraction and repulsion, even less comprehended than the man himself, and all the while she was going on living in the outward conditions of her old life. . . . [B]ut this new life was not yet, and she could not even picture it clearly to herself. There was only anticipation, the dread and joy of the new and the unknown.

This sums it up. I'm about to enter a supposedly glorious new phase, choosing this one guy over all the other guys in the world, leaving my old life to start a new one, but still nothing has changed. I have the same stupid job, the same pile of laundry in the bedroom, the same haircut. Nicky and I have been together for almost three years, so we've hashed out a lot of issues that have to do with existing in the same (small) space, like our system for writing down phone messages and a way to match his obsessive tidiness with my innate inability to screw on lids or put away shoes. Yet these are only superficial adjustments to a life together that I know is going to be completely transformed, either by our careers, or by starting a family, or by getting old. I'm just not sure what kind of expectations to have about this marriage, or whether I should even have any in the first place. I can feel changes coming, but I can't see what they're going to be.

In the meantime, I'm sick of getting rejection letters from nineteen-year-old interns at literary magazines. Yesterday I received a page-long letter from an earnest girl named Bambi or something, telling me that she discerned some talent in my work but would I consider turning my play into a short story, changing the title and setting, and cutting out all the characters? This has got to be some sort of karmic punishment for all the dashed-off rejection letters I wrote during my past life in publishing. I wish I could take them all back and rewrite them to sound a little more intelligent—or at least a little more kind.

FEBRUARY

I dream about her more often than I think about her during the day. Sometimes in the dreams she is the way she used to be, alert, engaged, and funny. Other times she forgets something obvious, like where she keeps her sweaters, or whether she's ever been to Spain, and I suddenly remember (because in the dream I am the one who has forgotten that she's sick), and it hits me like the first time.

This morning I woke up crying but had no recollection of a dream, just a wet pillow. Work days after something like this are always a lost cause, because I can't act as if nothing has happened—although nothing, of course, actually has. I try to go on as usual, but I feel tired and defeated. Today I watched TV for a couple hours in the morning instead of writing anything. I feel screwed up.

What makes her disease so difficult for me to accept is that she doesn't accept it herself. Despite the letter from the doctor, and the fact that she is willingly taking medication, she still insists that there is nothing wrong. If I happen to catch her in the act, like when I drove her into town and she couldn't tell me the way to the grocery store, she makes up an excuse. It's because Dad never lets her drive so she never learned the way, or she just got distracted by the conversation. She has never come close to admitting that she's aware of acting differently than before.

I've got the number of a therapist on my desk, someone who specializes in everything to do with memory diseases, including helping people whose mothers have them, but I'm still thinking about whether to call. The only other shrink I've seen confused me. I kept saying, "I want to be creative, I want to write, I don't know how to start," and she would mull it over and say, "How about advertising?" She didn't understand that what I wanted was to live a totally different life. Anyway, I started to lie to her to try to make her happy, and I'd tell her how I was looking into advertising as a career. That was the beginning of the end. If I wanted to lie to someone for fifty minutes, I figured I could do that for free.

So if I make this call and go to see this therapist, what will I be lying about now? That I can handle this sorrow? That marriage is going to make things better? That my mother is in denial and I am not?

$\sim$

It's only mid-February and already I'm knee-deep in wedding plans. We know this much: it's going to take place on September 6 on Martha's Vineyard (where Nicky lived half the time as a kid), and we're going to have it outside. I have met with two tent companies and a caterer, and we have appointments with a photographer, a cake baker, and an invitation maker next week.

The funny thing about meeting with these people is

they all treat you like you're a potentially violent mental patient. For example, last weekend Nicky, his mom, and I went to see the tent lady in her office. The tent lady is responsible for renting out most of the equipment we need for the wedding: tables, chairs, silverware, lights, napkins, serving dishes, and so on. For just about everything, she had three choices: there was the cheapo cafeteria fork, the faux-elegant-but-still-tacky version, and finally, the heavy, perfectly balanced restaurant fork. Needless to say, the more decent the fork, the more expensive. Tent Lady sat across from us with a clipboard in her hand, asking us questions about what we wanted and taking notes in triplicate on a special form. Whenever I made any kind of correction, like asking for smaller tables or a larger dance floor, she would look at me, her eyes sparkling with can-do spirit, compliment me on my foresight, and cautiously explain how she might accommodate my wishes. As if she'd never heard anyone suggest a larger dance floor before. I started to realize that this was an ongoing phenomenon when, after asking what I thought was a simple question, the fourth or fifth vendor said to me, "It's *your* day. It's up to *you*."

I'm not used to being the center of fawning attention like this, and frankly I don't like it. At the first meetings, the vendors act as if working at my wedding is the most special job they've ever been asked to do; but of course, they've done a million weddings before mine and are going to do them exactly the way they're used to doing them. So in subsequent discussions, if I request something slightly different from what they're used to, everyone rolls their eyes and I end up feeling like a classic Bitchy Bride. I try not to take it personally. What I should do is enjoy the power while I have it. When else am I going to get to throw such a party? This *it's-your-day* mantra makes sense. Let the bastards eat cake!

This is the crux of my problem so far with planning my wedding: the romance of getting married and the day-dream of a perfect day have nothing to do with the work that it takes to make a wedding come together. I want to sail into this wedding with the same giddy excitement which I had when I fell in love, but moronic tasks and tricky questions intervene. About money, for example. I know a lot of couples pay for their own weddings these days, but our parents have offered to each pay half, and we're not about to object. It wasn't a difficult decision to make: we both wanted to have a big, fun wedding, and we couldn't have done it on our own. But with accepting our parents' help, we also take on the task of finding some kind of middle ground between the styles of our two families, as well as incorporating our own style, so that everyone can be happy. This seems slightly impossible, but we'll see. A friend described this process as playing the princess but always feeling the pea. It's true. No matter how lucky I feel, how magical this time is, there's always something. The pea is big. The pea is persistent. The pea is everywhere.

~

Nicky's parents have decided to throw us a big engagement party. I know that, according to the wedding etiquette rule books, this is technically the bride's family's domain, but since I'd never even heard of an engagement party before this, and since we are already turning tradition on its head by having the wedding at the groom's house and doing most of the planning with the groom's mother, I'm unconcerned about our latest infraction. My father has asked to pay for our dinner, and I've decided to leave it at that. To be frank, Nicky's family has more money than mine, as far as I can tell; and although his parents have solid, middle-class values and down-to-earth styles, and mine have done well enough to now retire in comfort, they are—on paper, at least—from two different walks of life. Therefore, I'm trying not to fixate on making everything perfectly equal; instead I'm concentrating on the more pressing fact that my parents will be meeting Nicky's parents for the first time.

With my folks being in New Hampshire and only coming to the city a couple times a year, it's worked out that they haven't met before. I am nervous; our parents couldn't be more different from one another. My parents live in the mountains and Nicky's live in Manhattan. Jill and John have dinner at six; Betsy and Davis have dinner at nine. It's as if they're two different species of humans—although for a while there you might have thought they were exactly the same. Both families raised their children mostly in the comfortable suburbs of New York City and sent their kids to good colleges. Both families chose travel over new cars, dinners at home over restaurants. But somehow, now that my parents have moved deeper into the country and Nicky's have moved back to the city, they seem a world apart, country mice and city mice. I have to keep reminding myself that Nicky and I are getting married, not our parents.

By the way, I can never say "fiancé." The word screams out for attention, for a follow-up question, a demand of proof: a date, a chosen location, a sizable diamond in a tasteful setting. It's so cheesy-sounding, with its French swoop. Whenever I hear it, I picture Nicky with a beret and a little mustache. I never know what to say when I introduce him anymore, so I stammer and hedge and sound like an idiot. My sweet *croissant*, I should call him. My darling *café au lait*.

I'm not sure where this aversion comes from. Maybe I actually like the way it sounds but don't want to admit it. I'm constantly torn between being thrilled about getting married and wondering if I'm getting a bit *too* involved. Is it creepy to be so excited? Logically, I know that being a bride does not preclude my being a feminist. However, I have noticed that I am doing most of the planning of the "girl stuff," from selecting food to choosing ribbons to calling about decorations, and Nicky is doing the "guy stuff," like talking to the band, renting the toilets, and staking out tent space in the yard. Sometime I have a feeling I should be doing things differently, just to show that I'm a totally liberated gal. I should pee in the yard or fix a tractor or something. But the truth is that I'm totally into what I'm doing—God help me—down to the last canapé and frosted flower.

~

Today I went shopping with Betsy to choose stuff for my registry. I had been dead set against registering—it seemed old-fashioned and kind of crass to me. What did I need with silver knives and forks? How can I demand that people buy me only those presents I'm sure to like? But I went along with her, mainly because it sounded like so much fun to go to Tiffany's and Bloomingdale's with Nicky's mom. I enjoyed how normal we must have looked to the people around us—a mother and daughter trolling through the housewares department, debating the virtues of nonstick pans and the necessity of a good set of knives. Feeling that reminded me that Betsy is not my mother, which in turn made me feel guilty for wishing my mother were more like Betsy. Which, of course, she never was.

When Mom got engaged in 1964, she was a stewardess for TWA. At the time it was a very glamorous job—she wore a short bolero jacket over a sleek shift dress, high heels, and a little round hat. She met Dad, who at the time was working for Esso as an engineer, on a date in

New York that was set up by their parents at home in England. He was smoking a pipe at the hotel bar when she walked in with a bunch of her girlfriends, all stewardesses, all in uniform, their regulation scarves knotted around their necks. Just before she got married, my mother dropped into a department store in New York and bought her wedding dress in one day, without any help from her mother, who was across the ocean in England. They returned to England for their wedding, which was at a local church, and the reception was at a restaurant across the street. Kind of makes what I'm planning seem excessive by comparison. But fun, too.

It's hard for me not to be doing this the Jill Beesley way, especially now, because I feel like I should be honoring her. But I don't want to buy a wedding dress without any help, and I like having Betsy call me with a new thought on the smoothest transition from ceremony to dinner or tell me about a great store where we can buy ribbon at a discount. I'm not sure if this is confusing to me because Mom is sick, or because I'm choosing a different kind of life from the one that she chose for herself. As I am her only daughter, should I not be more her daughter? If I could get up the guts to ask her, and if she could magically articulate an answer, would she say that my choices dismay her? Or does she understand and accept that in my being so different from her, she has fulfilled a sort of American dream by rearing a typically American child? I do know this: if she were there at Tiffany's, she would have had one look at the price of a silver fork and demanded to know what was wrong with stainless steel.

After walking around the department stores with Betsy, I decided I *liked* the silver knives and forks, concluded I *wanted* a Cuisinart, and figured if people wanted to buy them for me, I ought to make the choice easy for them.

Long live the Bitchy Bride.

MARCH

Every Wednesday, between seven and nine, I call Mom, because that's when Dad goes out for his regular date to play the violin in a small string group. Mom knows that I am getting married, but she doesn't remember when. I think she's afraid she's going to miss it, because she always says on the phone, over and over, that she hopes it will be soon. She can often recall all the names in our new extended family, even Emma's, but she mixes up pronouns, like "him" and "her," "he" and "she." She usually couldn't tell you what she did earlier that day, whether she ate lunch or went for a walk, but she often remembers all the words to a favorite old song, and can name the artist and sing the chorus after the first few notes come on the radio.

I've learned to avoid asking her a lot of questions, which seems to make her anxious. Somehow she must know that she's not going to respond properly, and so she freezes up. The problem is, once you rule out questions in a conversation, there's not a whole lot left, except to tell stories, which is what I do. I tell her everything I've done during the week, repeating things she's already heard if I feel like it. I tell her that my writing is going well, that I saw Julia for dinner, that Sonya has a new job, that Elliot is moving to California. I tell her about a movie I saw and about what I had for dinner. When I run out of things to tell her, she usually comes up with a few half-stories for me. I've heard most of them before: there's one about the guy who came to fix the chimney, and another about a hot air balloon that flew over the backyard. Sometimes there will be a new story, but usually I have to wait to get all the details from my father before I understand exactly what happened.

There's something almost nice about being able to talk so freely, to chat without context and without having to avoid digressions or make some scintillating point, but these conversations are never easy, mostly because as soon as I hang up the phone, I wonder if I could have done a better job of it. I beat myself up for not making her laugh, or for inadvertently asking a question she can't answer, or for talking too little or too much. The good news is that Nicky usually gets home soon afterward, pours us both a glass of wine, and tells me that I'm a great daughter and that she loves me, and that he does too.

My father says that even on other nights when I call, Mom will look up from whatever she's doing as the phone is ringing and say, "That must be Mandy." And she's always right.

~

My parents are coming this weekend. Not only will Saturday night be the first time our parents meet, but Sunday is the big, Manhattan-style engagement party that Nicky's parents are throwing in our honor. My dad has been calling all week with questions about what to wear, what to bring the Weinstocks for a present, and whether he'll be expected to make a toast. I have all the answers: jacket and tie, some flowers, and no, a speech is not required. My being nervous is probably rubbing off on him. I wish I knew how to be poised and graceful throughout this drama, but I'm too excited to act like this kind of thing happens to me every day.

Nicky and I have been trying to figure out what kind of restaurant we should choose for our first all-family dinner. We wanted something nice but not glitzy, quiet but not staid, festive but not fancy, not too country and not too city. I instructed him to tell his dad that my father would pick up the dinner check, a simple request that I had built up in my imagination as a big deal. It wasn't. These negotiations seemed a lot harder in the abstract than they were in practice, but for a while I was on pins and needles. Nicky is nervous, too, only less so than I am. It doesn't come just from putting our families together, although that is a big part of it. This is also the beginning of formally announcing our engagement to the world. If the dinner makes me nervous, the engagement party threatens to be overwhelming. The last party for me was my sweet sixteen, and that was ten girls on the back porch drinking weak champagne punch out of paper cups. And we thought *that* was a party. Try putting your high school friends, your college friends, your work friends, your parents, and your parents' friends in the same room and telling them to have fun in your honor. I wonder if they'll still have it if I call in sick.

~

Sometimes I get nervous that people will be put off by Mom when they first meet her, because she looks and acts totally fine until you ask her when she arrived, where she came from, or whether she's ever been there before. It's not until she attempts to answer that you realize she doesn't quite know. I've noticed that as soon as people learn that she's got memory problems, they're much more comfortable with her; but that doesn't make it any easier for me to tell people.

Fortunately, Nicky's folks were well prepared for the first time everyone met. We decided that we should have a pre-first-meeting meeting on Saturday afternoon, so we arranged to go for a walk in Central Park. Betsy brought their dog, Harry, and we brought Emma. The dogs went charging off together, and something about the animals getting along so well made the humans among us follow suit.

Afterward we went to Nicky's family's apartment for tea—or wine for the New Yorkers. As soon as we walked in, Mom announced that she had been in the apartment before. This happens fairly often when she's in a new place, and Dad will usually gently remind her that she must be thinking of somewhere else. But before that could happen, Betsy replied, "Yes, and don't you love these old buildings?" And off they went into a discussion, of sorts, about New York architecture. We muddled through an hour of chatting, Dad presented Davis and Betsy with a perfectly beautiful window box full of flowers, and then we went home to get ready for dinner.

The funny thing about her thinking she'd been there before is that none of us *really* knew if it was true or not. Mom lived in New York for a year or so when she was working as a stewardess. It could very well be that she went to a party or knew someone who had an apartment in the building—and there's no reason why anyone would know except for her.

Later we met for dinner at a French bistro uptown. It was all very funny and sweet. My mother couldn't figure out what to order, and once she decided, she forgot what she had chosen. Nicky's father mysteriously started speaking with a British accent. Dad couldn't hear across the table and made a few crazy guesses at answers rather than asking anyone to repeat the question. Betsy talked about a French writer none of us had heard of. I kept butting in and answering for everyone else, and Nicky was oddly quiet. But it was OK, and more important, we had made the first gesture of bringing the families together. I understood that our parents were not going to come out of this as doubles partners, and they didn't; but they genuinely liked one another, had some good conversations and real laughs, and tried as hard as they could, for our sake, to make it work. I guess part of me wanted them to fall in love the way Nicky and I had fallen in love, but this was good enough. More than that, it was the way it was supposed to be.

My father paid for dinner, Betsy and my mom talked a bit about their own weddings, and Nicky and I leaned into each other, holding hands under the table.

~

My parents took off this morning, back to the land of frozen lakes and snowshoes. The engagement party was swish, over-the-top, staggering, and exciting. I felt thrilled and embarrassed by all the attention, which seemed undeserved; we weren't about to climb Mt. Everest or anything, we were just getting hitched. But I should start at the beginning. I bought a dress for the occasion, a long, lavender cotton sheath with a slit up the back. By the time we got out of the taxi, I was a wrinkled mess. Nicky's brother

Luke rescued me from hyperventilating: he handed me some sweats and ironed my dress while I sat numbly on the couch. By the time I put the dress back on, the first guests began to arrive. I was so wound up I was forgetting names of people I'd known all my life. I had dementia—I *knew* it—but then, after a glass of wine, it went away. The caterers went out of their way to bring me firsts of all the hors d'oeuvres. The funniest was a young man, about five feet tall, who kept popping up in front of me and saying, "Shrimp?"

Halfway through the evening, Nicky's father made a toast. It was all about me, how great I am, how happy they are to have me as part of the family: their first daughter. I was dizzy with compliments. When he had finished, and the crowd's gaze swerved to me, waiting expectantly for the grandiloquent response to come, I raised my glass and said, dumbly, "Thanks."

Smooth. It was all I could think of at the time.

Toward the end of the night, Mr. Donohue, my parents' friend from New Jersey, went out to the coatrack to get his overcoat and found that it was gone. I couldn't believe it—his coat, stolen! I took the theft as a symbol of my new life, a gaudy city life of fancy engagement parties, suits and ties, coatracks and caterers. For a sickening moment it seemed as though the whole wedding were going to fall apart. Nicky found me outside the apartment, frantically looking through the coats, and convinced me that there must have been a mistake. Of course, this morning I got a call from the Donohues. They had left the coat in the car and never hung it on the rack in the first place.

Now that it's all over, I'm ashamed of myself for worrying about what my parents would think of Nicky's parents, and what Nicky's parents would think of mine—as if any of them would be anything but warm toward the others. Still I wondered whether my parents thought I was giving up the life they'd taught me to live by joining forces with this new family, and I wondered whether Nicky's parents were looking at me and wondering the same thing. Of course, no one was thinking anything of the sort. And for that matter, Nicky's family isn't so different from my own. Coming together hasn't diluted us; rather, it has made us more sturdily ourselves.

Still, seeing our parents together—that is, seeing where we came from—it made me aware of how much thought must go into deciding what we will try to take from our family legacies and what we will desperately try to leave behind.

~

My ring has been sliding around more than ever and scratching up the skin on my third finger. I recently decided that having it made smaller might make it more stable, so I quietly brought it to the place where Nicky bought it. They warned me that changing the ring might weaken the setting (whatever that meant), but they went

59

ahead and resized it for me. It felt a little better—but then last night as I talked on the phone, I idly twisted the ring around on my finger and the damned diamond fell right out!

I had to tell Nicky. We sat down on the couch, and I calmly told him what had happened. He told me to give him the ring and said that he would take care of it. Thinking that we were about to plan a strategy together, I suggested a few people who might know good jewelers, then told him which days I would be free to help choose a setting. A look passed over his face that I don't see very often, one of steely determination and controlled fury. I asked him what was wrong.

"Let me take care of this, OK?" he asked, getting up. It was unusual for him to end a discussion so abruptly, and I didn't know what to say next. I knew that he had purchased the diamond from a jeweler who was a friend of his family, then designed a setting himself and commissioned another jeweler to make it. It had been far more complicated a process than going to Tiffany's and buying a ring. I think he saw it as his first herculean test of being a husband, and it made him angry, or scared, or frustrated, or all three, not to have passed with flying colors.

What I realized, as I got ready for bed, is how differently we reacted to the broken ring. Whereas my impulse was for us to talk about the problem and then come up with a solution together, Nicky simply wanted to take the thing and fix it. My way seemed to make more sense, since it would take some of the pressure off Nicky to find the right jeweler, choose a new setting, and make sure it was done safely and quickly. It would also be a chance for us to attack a problem together, as a team. At the same time, I felt I owed it to him to at least try this his way, since it was so clearly what he wanted. That night in bed, once I'd turned the lights out, I told him that if he wanted me to help, I would, but that otherwise I wouldn't ask him about it. He said, once again, that he wanted to take care of it himself, then kissed me good night. I turned the light back on. "Can I say one more thing?" I asked. "I just want to remind you that this ring is a symbol, but it's not an omen. Don't think that a weak ring is the sign of a weak marriage, OK?"

Nicky grunted what I took as agreement, and I turned out the light again.

~

For months I've been quietly writing away but not actually *doing* anything with the stuff I've written. It finally occurred to me that no one was going to magically discover my work until I put some of it into the world. Having had little success with short fiction, I decided to try my hand at magazine writing. I made an appointment with an editor at *Self* magazine, and yesterday I met her to talk about an idea I had for an article about getting engaged. The editor had my proposal letter in her hand when I entered her office. I sat down, and after exchanging a few pleasantries, she gently told me she didn't think my idea was quite right for the magazine.

I felt ridiculous. Why had she called me in just to reject me? What did she mean it wasn't right? Was I so off base that they couldn't make it right? I hurriedly thanked her for the meeting and reached for my bag. I half stood up, then realized that she wasn't waiting for me to leave. She told me about the magazine's readership and described some upcoming articles. Then we walked around the office, and she introduced me to a few members of the editorial staff. As she steered me to the elevator, told me she liked my writing, and encouraged me to try her again, I understood that she actually meant she'd like to see more of my writing. I was walking on clouds for the rest of the day.

~

That night I dreamed I had lost one of my shoes. I came across a new shoe and put it on, but it didn't quite fit. With this new shoe on one foot and my old shoe on the other, I limped and staggered, unable to move forward.

What is this shoe that doesn't fit? What are the two worlds I'm trying to reconcile? Is it about calling myself a writer when I still haven't convinced myself that I can succeed? Is it about my wedding and this role of bride that I'm not so sure really suits me? Or perhaps it's that I'm not

Cinderella, as I thought when I tried on dresses, but instead I'm one of the evil stepsisters (only this sister still hasn't found a gown for the ball). And what about the shoe that I lost? I wonder if it really was a new shoe, or if I've just outgrown the old one. Maybe this has to do with becoming a mother to my own mother. I may still be a daughter, but the role is getting bigger, and I'm feeling squeezed.

Then again, it could just be the odd dream about footwear.

APRIL

Today I was talking to Karen on the phone, and she referred to a day ten years ago when my mother picked us up from college in Manhattan and drove us home to New Jersey, where we all lived.

I asked, "You mean she drove in by herself from New Jersey?"

"Sure," she said. "I remember it was snowing."

I was surprised; I didn't remember it at all. It seemed incredible to me that Mom could have accomplished such a feat. That part of my mother is gone, the woman who could negotiate the traffic and highway mazes of the Garden State, find her way to Manhattan and then to 116th and Broadway to pick up her daughter and her daughter's friend from college. I wish I could remember what we talked about. I wonder if I asked her how her day was, or complained about a class I was taking, or argued with her about the best route home. The thing about her loss of memory is that it constantly challenges my own, and I always feel panicked, as though I'm starting to lose it too.

My memories are undeniably confused; I have trouble separating the mother Mom really was from the mother I wanted her to be—or want her, now, to have been. When I sit around feeling cheated by this illness, angry that she's not able to help plan this wedding, or to give me advice on my career, or to tell me everything I need to know about men and marriage, I'm lying to myself. These are all things she wouldn't have done anyway, sick or not. When I start to feel sorry for myself, the person I'm really missing is some kind of perfect Glenda the Good Witch, giving me all the things a child could possibly expect from a mother, which of course no mother can actually give.

What I want more than anything is one more glimpse at the way she used to be—a nighttime tour with the Ghost of Christmas Past—so that I can put make-believe to rest for good.

∼

Lately I am out of my mind with in-betweens: spending money I don't have, working in a stupid job I'll eventually quit, starting a career I have no idea I can survive in, living in an apartment I'm dying to move out of, juggling appointments with priests and Porta-John companies. The only definite thing in my life is that Nicky and I are getting married on September 6, and that I'm going to need every second between now and then to get ready.

I find I'm complaining all the time. On the phone last night my brother Tony said he was worried by how much I worry. He said I had to calm down about all the planning, that it would eventually work out. But this wedding stuff isn't the same for guys, no matter who they are or how much they try to help. I have to give him credit, though; he's been really helpful to me in talking about Mom. I know he thinks about her a lot and wants to help, although there's only so much he can do from Seattle. Come to think of it, there's not so much anyone can do from anywhere.

∼

Today I was walking to the grocery store and I passed Jordan, who was sitting on the curb, surrounded by several cans of paint and hard at work transforming the dull gray fire hydrant in front of our building into a work of art. (On the Lower East Side you can do that kind of thing without getting arrested for defacing public property.) Jordan lives in the apartment downstairs. She is one of those people you have to hate: beautiful, funny, carefree, always smiling. Today, as usual, the sun was shining just for Jordan, and she was paying it back by decorating the street. By the time I returned, the three hydrants on our block were painted in bold happy colors, and she had begun to spread her cheery artistry across to the next block.

The whole perfect picture of it made me furious, sullen, frustrated. I realized I was envious. She had seen something she wanted to do, something creative, and she did it. And now every time she walked down the street she would be reminded of her success, and I would be reminded to ask myself what I've done lately. It has something to do with her courage and her industry, neither of which I feel like I have these days. All this anxiety comes from my new theory that there isn't quite enough good luck or success to go around. So if Julia Roberts is making $16 million a picture, or if a girl I knew at college just married a millionaire, or if Jordan is painting the hydrants, then my chances for any kind of happiness are made that much slimmer.

I should add that on her evening walk, showing off acute canine psychic abilities, Emma dragged me to one of the newly painted hydrants, squatted right next to it, and peed.

~

OK, so sex last night was not so hot. Let's just say Nicky's train left the station without me. I wasn't even on my way to the station. I hadn't even started to pack my bags. To be fair, it wasn't really his fault; for whatever reason, I deliberately failed to communicate what I was feeling. It was as if I wanted it to be awkward. Sex is usually easy between us, and on the occasions when it hasn't been perfect, we've always laughed about it afterward. This time, though, I was determined not to laugh it off, and further determined to let Nicky feel bad about it.

Whenever something goes wrong nowadays, whether it be a rejection letter from a magazine, or a bounced check, or a bad night in bed, instead of seeing it as an anomaly, I see it as an omen. A really bad one. It feels as if, on the brink of marriage, all things are poised to be set in stone— the mistakes and shortcomings a permanent part of my life, whereas before they were simply harmless blunders. One night of mediocre sex suddenly suggests a whole life of it. I know I'm wrong about this. I could have a little faith in the triumph of good over bad. It wouldn't kill me.

∼

Despite Nicky's and my efforts to make planning this wedding a joint venture, I've realized that the joint is ultimately made up of me and Betsy. I can give Nicky assignments, like to arrange for the booze to be dropped off or to send a map to the band, and he does them cheerfully; but the fact is that he's not going to wake up in the middle of the night worrying about the wedding the way I do. I think that's what I was so angry about the other night in bed. I was answering his apathy with some of my own. A very manipulative response, and one that didn't do any good, but there it is.

It's hard to pin him down on his passivity, because it's not as if he's been watching football games with his buddies while I've been meeting with the caterer. He has been with me all along; he's just not as obsessed with it all as I am. *It's your day*, the professionals keep chirping, and I have started to believe them. But why? How can marriage today still be so much more about the bride than the bridegroom? To the rest of the world, our wedding may appear less bride-centric, I suppose, considering it's taking place in Nicky's backyard; but still I can feel the weight of tradition bearing down to make this all about me.

I have to keep reminding myself that our wedding and our marriage are two completely different things. Nicky's lack of initiative in planning the wedding has nothing to do with the way he's going to act as a husband. He shows plenty of initiative in other ways, like when he read about the Van Gogh exhibit in Washington and then arranged for us to drive down and see it. Or the time he decided our books and CDs should be reorganized and spent a weekend classifying and alphabetizing them. It doesn't matter to me whether the fiction is separate from the poetry, or whether the jazz is mixed with the pop, so I didn't help. Maybe from Nicky's perspective, this wedding is a giant alphabetizing project that he's involved with only because it matters to me. It's still annoying, but I guess this is the only wedding we'll ever have, so I don't have to worry about it becoming a pattern.

It's my *day*. Not my *life*.

~

Today Nicky presented me with a new and improved engagement ring. It was fun opening the box, like getting engaged all over again. I suggested that maybe he should go out and find a new setting a couple times a year, and he chased me around the apartment and tackled me on the sofa.

~

I tried on Nicky's grandmother's wedding dress this afternoon, an ivory silk gown from the 1920s with a lace jacket that went over it. I liked the idea of being able to carry on a family tradition, and it would also have saved me a bundle. But as I modeled it in front of the mirror, I realized that it wasn't my dream dress, whatever that is. I don't think Betsy cared either way, but I was still sorry I couldn't do the honor to her mother.

My mother's dress was beautiful, or at least she looked beautiful in it in all the pictures: it had short sleeves, a round neckline, and little white daisies embroidered on the skirt. There was nothing about that dress I didn't like, except maybe for the lace starfish contraption that held her veil on her head. When I was a teenager, it occurred to me after school one day that the dress was there in the house and I had never actually seen it. I asked her if I could try it on, and she said OK, so I dragged the big gray plastic blob of its casing out of the attic and into my bedroom. When I opened it up and looked at the dress, I found that it was not in good shape: the silk had yellowed in places, and the little appliquéd flowers on the skirt were falling off. It was also too small—there was no way it would zip up my back.

At the time, my mother was working downstairs. When I think about it now, it occurs to me that if it were *my* daughter trying on *my* wedding dress, I'd want to be there to see what it looked like twenty years later, even if it looked awful on her. I'm not sure why she skipped this sentimental opportunity. Maybe it's because, contrary to what I'd like to believe, her world did not completely revolve around me. It could also be that her wedding day didn't mean so very much to her.

My father once told me that their wedding celebration in England, in 1965, reflected their parents' taste and choices far more than it did their own. He said that's how everyone did it back then. I guess what we're doing, or trying to do, is somewhere in between us and our parents. We want to invite plenty of our own friends, but we want our parents to have friends there as well. We want music that the "young people" can dance to, but we don't want to alienate the grown-ups. We want a ceremony performed by a minister, but we don't want to be hypocritical about the fact that neither of us goes to church. The thing is, it's not my day, or our day; it's *everybody's* day. Once we're married and things have settled down, then all the days will finally be ours.

~

Nicky's dad just had an operation to have his knee replaced. We visited him in the hospital today. For the first time it seemed important that we were engaged. I still would have gone to the hospital even if we weren't, but this was different. I can't explain it. It just was. I felt responsible for his family, and part of his family, in a way I never have before.

MAY

I'm Michelle's maid of honor for her wedding on May 10—my debut as a bridesmaid, and I'm not sure exactly what I'm supposed to do. One thing I *have* picked up (the foot-in-mouth way, as usual) is that you don't yammer on about your own wedding with your friend who's getting married in less than a week. Why I couldn't have figured this out ahead of time, I don't know, but there I was with Michelle, working out the final hysterical moments of travel details and bridesmaid duties, when I found myself saying things like "Wow, these are the exact same flowers I'm planning to use at my wedding!" and "Do you think I should have a printed menu at my wedding too?" What's wrong with me? Who the hell fails Bridesmaid 101?

Michelle didn't actually say anything about my gaffes; in fact, she may not have noticed them at all. I'm finding it hard to read her right now, in the midst of her prewedding flurry. Then again, I'm probably not as good at reading her as I was in high school and for several years after that, when we spent lazy summers together, driving around town, lying on the driveway and chewing tobacco for the first (and only) time, drinking Diet Cokes and eating ice cream in her family's living room. I think I'm still imagining that she's that same Michelle of our childhood, *my* Michelle, who stood on the sofa and sang along with Sheena Easton on her eight-track player. She's not, of course, just as I am not the same teenager who put a pillow under her shirt and tried (unsuccessfully) to buy beer at the local liquor store. Time for me to let go of that image and embrace this new one: Michelle as a bride, a wife, my married friend, who can buy beer anytime she wants but who these days prefers white wine. I see that she's different now, stronger and more confident, deeply in love with Ray, excited to move on in her new life. This doesn't mean our friendship is over, but I am beginning to understand that it has to change, whether I want it to or not.

This realization has been a long time coming. When Michelle called me eight months ago to tell me that Ray had proposed to her, and that she wanted me to be her maid of honor, I burst into tears. Of course I was happy for her—Ray is an exceptional man, smart and kind, and I know he will be a good husband—but my happiness for her came with a sense of personal loss. She was starting off on a journey, and it was one that I wouldn't be taking with her. So much for our own childhood trips to the Jersey shore, and visiting each other at college in New York and Dallas. This was the big time, and although I was deeply involved with Nicky and expecting to marry him someday (this was five months before we got engaged), I couldn't help feeling that Michelle was leaving me behind. In many respects, this leave-taking was merely symbolic—she would still be living nearby, and I knew we would stay friends—but in others it was very, very real. Michelle and I, in our old incarnation as the closest of friends, were a thing of the past. Her engagement was proof that she has a new friend and traveling companion, the love of her life. Now, with my own wedding just four months away, I can't help but see myself in her, and I wonder if my own leave-taking will feel as dramatic to my unmarried friends.

I know how self-centered this is, but I can't help it. As the days speed toward Michelle's wedding, I find myself thinking constantly about my own, and obsessing over every aspect of what is about to come.

~

While I've been wasting my time on guest lists and honeymoon plans, my friend Julia has spent the past year making a movie. Last night it was shown at a theater downtown as part of a series of short films. Hers was by far the best: funny, smart, and brave. There were all kinds of people there to watch it, people I didn't know Julia knew, and as it turned out, she didn't know a lot of them either. They were strangers who liked her work.

I am very impressed with her. Not unreasonably jealous this time, like I was of Jordan, but moved and proud that she came up with an idea for something and followed through with it. My whole wedding saga suddenly seems kind of dull next to making a movie. I can't help thinking that marriage should be simple and quiet and meaningful, and so far planning one has been anything but that. Maybe I should make a movie of my wedding: a gritty, grainy documentary, with a handheld camera and noir lighting. Maybe I should paint our getaway car and all the other cars on the block. Maybe I should get a life.

~

Back from Michelle's wedding, which doubled as a reunion of a bunch of old friends from Mendham High, my Jersey alma mater. The night before the wedding, we all sat outside, smoking cigarettes and drinking wine. When Sue (whom I hadn't seen in at least two years) asked about my family, I told her for the first time about my mother's dementia. It was hard to talk about it. Sue was a huge part of my childhood, part of the clean and happy memories I have of being young. It felt strangely adult to talk about my mother in this way, to acknowledge that we are all older and more frightened, and that maybe even in that warm childhood the seeds of bad things to come were growing. It was sad, too. In a way it felt as though I were betraying a family secret, and I felt ashamed. And then ashamed of being ashamed.

When I was in grade school, my mother was a constant source of embarrassment for me. Like the time she won a downhill ski race in a bikini and her picture appeared on the front page of the local paper. Or when she talked to strangers in elevators. Or when she came with us to the Grateful Dead show at the Meadowlands because she wanted to hear them live. Now I think all these things are cool. I wish I could ski fast in a bikini. I wish I still liked going to outdoor concerts.

As I've said, she was different from the other mothers in town. She was crazy about birds and horses. Whenever she had a pencil in her hand, she would make little sketches on old envelopes and shopping lists. The picture would always be of a horse, and perched on the horse's back she would draw a little bird. I've always thought of my mother as that bird, shy and proud. And even fierce sometimes.

In our old house in New Jersey, there was a back porch off the kitchen which was covered with a lattice of grape-vines. One year in early June, a couple of finches built a nest in the leaves near the kitchen window, and my mother and I watched as the babies hatched, their tiny brown faces peering out from the leaves. A couple weeks later, as we sat at the breakfast table, we saw a huge crow circle the nest and made a sudden dive at the baby birds. It missed, came up quickly, and began to circle again. In an instant, my mother was out the back door and on the porch, a stick clutched in her hand. The crow made a second dive, and this time robbed one of the babies from its nest. My mother chased the crow down the garden, waving the stick and yelling. For the rest of the day, she was inconsolable. It was her fault, she said. If she could only have gotten there sooner, she might have saved the chick.

A few weeks later we were having dinner, and the subject of gun control came up. "I wish I had a gun," said my sweet, nonviolent mother.

We turned to her in surprise. Someone asked why.

She looked out the window. "To shoot the crows," she said calmly.

The crow never got a second chance, anyway; my mother had us all watch the nest until every last bird learned to fly.

Mom never seemed to notice that she wasn't like most people on our street, that she cared more for finches than for block parties. I wonder how she would feel, how she does feel, to know that this disease makes her different in a different way, that sympathy now comes as often as admiration. I know my own feelings are a dizzying mixture of both.

∼

Things not to do at our wedding:

1. no kiss-then-hug at the altar (dead giveaway that the romance is already sagging)—must be *kiss only*.
2. no Louis Armstrong/Ella Fitzgerald numbers about the way I wear a hat
3. no readings from Dr. Seuss
4. no garter belt throwing
5. no cutesy photos of bride with babies
6. no Macarena, hokeypokey, or line dance to "Achy Breaky Heart"

∼

I dreamed I was at a big outdoor picnic and there was a show being performed by a bunch of monkeys. Watching the show nearby was a man I hadn't seen in a while, an ex-boyfriend. I pointed out to him that another old girlfriend of his was dancing near the stage. She was moving awkwardly, without grace or rhythm. The man told me he didn't recognize her, which made me sad. He told me he was about to get married. I leaned over and kissed him, then apologized for it. I thought about apologizing to his ex-girlfriend, too, but didn't.

Julia once told me that when you dream, you can find part of yourself in every character you encounter. I can see myself in the old girlfriend, dancing awkwardly and alone. I feel like that a lot of the time, and especially so with this wedding, where we're trying to turn something traditional into something personal and different. It's romantic, but it's also lonely. I am also the man in my dream, about to be married, leaving old loves behind. And I am myself, thinking about kissing an ex-boyfriend and disappointed that he doesn't even recognize me. Wondering where love goes when it's over.

Found out today that my play was rejected by another festival. I think I'm going to quit sending it out and try working on something else for a while.

~

I dreamed I saw my old boyfriend Kevin. We were in a strange building with a courtyard pool. I didn't tell him I was getting married at first, but then I did. It was a flicker of a dream, there and gone. I don't remember how he reacted or what happened next.

I've been thinking about Kevin lately, wondering where he is and whether I should call him to tell him that I'm getting married. I'm not sure what the etiquette is on this one. He was my boyfriend at the end of college, and we stayed together for three years after I graduated. It was, I suppose, my first adult relationship, although when I look back on those four years, I realize I was still a kid. We broke up a year before I met Nicky, and we haven't talked since. The breakup was painful and sad, not because we hated each other, but because we didn't: we just couldn't seem to figure out how to move forward together. Now, after nearly five years, I don't know whether he'd be glad to hear from me or not. I don't know anything about him. I think I won't call.

It's not easy to leave people in the past. It feels efficient, heartless.

~

Back from John and Deb's wedding. Nicky was the best man and delivered a speech that left not a dry eye in the house. I was so proud of him—he was really wonderful.

When we got home there was a message for Nicky with an offer from a book editor for a ghostwriting job. He proposed that we do it as a team so that I can get my name on a published book. I am thrilled, as it will be my first-ever writing job. It's not a lot of money but at least it's a start. It should take two months to finish, so I'll be done before our wedding. Best of all, I can quit working at the law firm and become a full-time professional writer.

The book is about bridge, as in the card game played by millions of senior citizens all over Florida. This bridge guru hopes to ride a tidal wave of young, hip, martini-swilling bridge players who will reinvigorate the game. Nicky and I are supposed to be the disciples who can send the message to the masses. We're going to learn how to play and record the lessons, then turn the lessons into a beginner's book for young swingers. I figure it may come in handy one of these days. Shouldn't every girl know how to play bridge in case she gets stuck on an overnight train or an ocean liner with nothing to do?

It's a little funny that they chose us, especially considering neither of us knows a thing about bridge. But I love card games, so I'm sure I'll like this.

JUNE

According to her papers, today is Emma's first birthday. Exactly nine months and one day ago, I arrived at Kennedy Airport from a weeklong trip. It was my birthday. Before I left, Nicky had promised to meet me and take me out for dinner on the way home. He was there, as promised, but we never made it to the restaurant. As we kissed and hugged, he whispered, "There's someone with me who wants to meet you." He opened his bag, and curled inside was a beautiful, red-ribboned puppy. We named her Emma, which is short for Emerson—as in Ralph Waldo, Nicky's favorite writer.

That's what I love about Nicky. He's always surprising me. Once, when we were dating, he came with me to look for a pair of shoes. I was in the market for loafers I could wear every day, but I got sidetracked by this pair of boots. They were made of smooth black leather, with super-high heels and a zip on the inside, something a sexy secret agent would wear. I tried them on and paraded around the store, feeling dangerous, but I decided they were too expensive and even more impractical—the kind of shoes you're not actually supposed to walk in if you don't want to bust a metatarsal—and I had been taught to spend my money more wisely than that. We left the store and I forgot all about it. A few days later Nicky asked for my opinion on a manuscript he had been given at work, and he handed me a box with a publisher's sticker on top. That night, when I opened the box to give it a read, the boots were inside.

But back to the dog. Our friends teased that this new acquisition was just practice for having a baby. I'm not sure about that, but we have learned a lot from sharing the responsibility of training a dog. I hope babies are not so difficult. At least they learn to talk after a while.

Although we spent the day showering Emma with rawhide bones and squeaky toys shaped like vegetables, she seemed to prefer her old Daily Growl, a plastic newspaper she's had since we got her. I could learn a lot from this dog.

~

My last day at the law firm! To mark the occasion I swiped a bunch of office supplies—an immature gesture that will cost me karma points in my next life, I'm sure. A few of the lawyers stopped by my desk to ask what I was going to do next and to wish me luck. God, it feels good to quit. Everyone should quit something at least once a year, just for that irreplaceable feeling of being totally in control of your life.

After work, I met Nicky across the street at the bar of the Palace Hotel to celebrate. We love going to hotel bars together. In a hotel bar you feel you could be anywhere, and anything could happen. Nicky had two martinis, and I drank champagne. We made fun of everyone we saw who was wearing a suit. Then we went home and ordered in some cheap Thai food. It was a perfect night.

We were quitting. We were joining. I felt happy that we were together.

~

(Martha's Vineyard)

Went to the Chilmark church for Sunday service. I wanted to go because the minister, Arlene, had agreed to marry us, and it seemed only fair, if she was coming to our house to marry us, that we go to her church a few times to get to know her a little better. Nicky and Betsy came as well, which turned out to be a good thing, because halfway into the service, I began to cry.

As usual, it happened during a part of the service called the Prayers of the People. This is when the congregation reads a prayer together for all the people in the world, for world leaders and the local minister, family and enemies, people living and dead. I find it exquisitely beautiful, especially the final section, where people in the congregation can stand up and ask for prayers for loved ones who are suffering. At this service, hearing an older man say that his wife was in the hospital with a broken hip, and then a woman asking us to pray for her neighbor with cancer, I felt excruciatingly aware of how much we all suffer, how much pain there is in the world. And there was something about having people speak so honestly about their sadness that made me face my own sadness about my mother, that knocked away all the padding I'd so carefully placed around my real feelings, and the floodgates opened. All I wanted was my mother's love, the fierce attentiveness she always had for all of her children. I missed her so much. Crying uncontrollably, I slipped out of the church and sat outside under a tree.

I waited there, swollen and snuffling, as the service wrapped up. I took deep breaths and tried to concentrate on how lucky I am that she will be with me at my wedding. Things could be much worse, I told myself. At least she is happy. She has my father. She can still walk for miles.

The thing about crying is it takes a little while to bounce back, and until you do, there's no way to cover it up; your body betrays you. As I was sitting there, an old lady walked by on the road. She glanced at me, took a few more steps, then turned around and asked, "Did you have a good cry?" I nodded, trying to return her smile. "Good for you," she said. "Now you'll feel better." I didn't really feel better. I felt as if I'd been picked up and turned inside out. I was exhausted. It's a good thing we're not getting married in a church. I'd probably have to leave halfway through my own wedding and go sit under a tree.

When the service ended, Nicky, Betsy, and I piled into the car. Nicky put his arm around me, and Betsy asked if, instead of going right home, I wanted to go for a walk around town. We drove to Menemsha and got something to drink—I was dying of thirst—and walked around until we were hungry for lunch. By the time we got back to the house, I was feeling better, although tired and extremely vulnerable, as if a layer of skin had been stripped away.

Nicky made me lunch, then set me up outside with a book and a cup of tea, his chair pulled up right beside me. All day he watched me, took care of me, gently nursed me back to my old self. It was a reminder of how much I depend on him, and how much he loves me, and how sure I am that we belong together.

(Back Home)

I wonder if I've reached a point, at twenty-nine years old, where I don't need to make any new friends. We were in Boston over the weekend for Dan and Erin's wedding (wedding number four of this Year of the Wedding) and there was a woman at my table whom I liked a lot. She was my age, a writer, and she lived in New York City. We talked all night about books, men, writing, everything. At the end of the night we exchanged phone numbers, with every intention of getting together. Now that I'm home, however, I realize that I'm not going to call her. It just feels as if getting to know someone new is too much work. I wonder if she will call me, and if she doesn't, will it be for the same reason? When I was single I used to try harder to make female friends, and now that I'm not I don't try so hard. I don't want to be some video-watching, couples-only married couple, but this must be how it happens. I can feel the dull pull of it already. Having said that, some nights, when our plans fall through, and Nicky and I end up in front of the television watching a bad movie and eating take-out, I can't imagine anything better.

JULY

Having decided to forgo the expense of a hired calligrapher, I wasted the whole day in search of the perfect pens to use to address the envelopes for our invitations. I went to three different stores and ended up spending almost sixty dollars on pens. What is wrong with me? Don't I have anything better to do? The wedding plans seem alternately well in hand and totally out of control. Today seemed a well-in-hand day, which is probably why I blew it by spending so much time and money on a few Magic Markers. I'm now used to having this take over my life.

The bridge book is turning out to be harder than I expected. The game itself, which I thought would be fast and exciting, turns out to be extremely complicated, with all these mathematical calculations you have to make before you even play a card. I'm hoping that I'll still catch on—I'm sure it will come to me eventually. Meanwhile, the Guru is getting impatient with me and keeps mentioning other students who learned the game in a matter of days.

I got a haircut today. It's too short. I look like a boy. An ugly boy with big hips.

~

Went away for the weekend with Karen, Sonya, Michelle, and Phoebe, my oldest friends in the world. It was billed as a little reunion, but they had schemed to make it my bachelorette party. We packed up Karen's car with supplies and drove to a cabin that Michelle had rented in upstate New Jersey. We cooked a huge dinner and had lots of drinks. Michelle, only a few months into her new marriage, had lots to say about what it all meant to her. In fact, after a few drinks, it turned out we all had too much to say. We got into a heated debate about cheating: Sonya and I claimed that no one could really say for sure that she would never cheat on her husband. Michelle insisted that she knew she would not, that it would never be worth it to her to hurt him like that. We countered that she was being too simplistic, that the real world isn't that cut-and-dried. She said if you really love someone you can do anything. Just as we started to get really annoyed with one another, Phoebe changed the subject by bringing out an armful of gifts, which included a water pistol shaped like a penis and a bridal-striptease ensemble, complete with G-string, tassels, and a garter. I was just looped enough to try the whole thing on.

As I write this, both Phoebe and Sonya are probably on their way to the drugstore to pick up the pictures they took of me standing outside the cabin, on top of the picnic table, wearing sneakers and my new G-string and brandishing my penis pistol. I have to remember, if I ever decide to run for public office, to make sure I'm still on good terms with Sonya and Phoebe.

~

I've been thinking about the fidelity question that came up over the weekend. At first I thought that Michelle was unrealistic to expect any couple to remain faithful for an entire marriage, especially these days when marriages are so fragile anyway. But the more I thought about it, and especially when I thought about the reverse—Nicky talking to his friends about not remaining faithful to me—I realized how devastating infidelity would be. In order to make a marriage last forever, you have to *expect* it to last forever. Sometimes I get sidetracked by all the grim statistics about marriage and divorce (especially when we heard recently that a couple we've known for a long time, whom we always held up as having a great marriage, are separating), but if Nicky and I want to beat those odds, we're going to have to stick to the rules we make up at the beginning of our marriage. Expecting to be true to each other isn't unrealistic at all; it's the most practical way—in fact, the only way—of making it work.

AUGUST

Went to Molly and Bjorn's wedding over the weekend. Now at wedding number five we're clearly starting to flag: leaving our hotel late, getting lost en route to the church, peeling into the parking lot and racing across the lawn, only to miss the bride's procession by a minute. What jerks.

At the reception, everyone at our table was either nearly or newly married. I felt like a cliché, but it was still fun: Bjorn is Swedish and so there were all kinds of funny songs and traditions to learn about as the reception went on. You always hear about Swedish women being good-looking, but these groomsmen were to die for.

~

I had my first fitting for my dress today. It looks great: it's sleeveless and fitted to just below the waist, then it explodes into a poofy, knee-length, petticoat-filled skirt. Not understated. Not elegant. And not simple. If I hear the word "simple" to describe a wedding dress one more time, I'm going to scream. Wedding dresses are not simple. They are expensive, complicated, and strange as all hell. Mine especially: it keeps changing every time I see the dressmaker. Today she's decided to cover it with wide stripes of all different kinds of lace. I told her to go for it.

I found the dress at a little boutique across the street from my apartment. I went in alone, tried it on, and told the woman who owned the store that it was exactly what I wanted. Turns out, after all, that I ended up finding my dress almost the same way my mother found hers.

~

Melanie and Evan got married yesterday—which makes six weddings so far this year. The next one we go to is our own. I'm glad this run is over, not for the usual gripes about it being expensive to travel to all these events, buy gifts for everyone, and pay for hotel rooms, but because it's exhausting to watch when you have one of your own looming large. I'm constantly on the lookout for the do's and don'ts that might make our wedding more unique. (A few do's: I liked that Melanie had both her parents walk her down the aisle. I liked that the caterers put plenty of food on each plate. And my favorite: that she and Evan made bottles of beer as wedding favors, with a sticker on each that said "I Do Brew.")

Melanie was decked out in a gorgeous 1940s Hollywood wedding gown that her uncle made for her (he designs costumes for the movies). When her father made his toast he made us all cry as he spoke about wishing his parents were alive to see Melanie get married. Everybody's wedding has something that makes it uniquely theirs. John and Deb did a wild tango for their first dance; Dan serenaded Erin with a Sinatra song; Michelle and Ray left their reception in a fishing boat; and Molly and Bjorn had all the guests doing shots of aquavit. At every wedding I feel as if I get a fleeting glimpse through a window into the couple's life, and just as I realize I'm seeing something new about them, the window gets closed again, and they're married. They become a bastion of privacy, a quietly fortified bunker that nobody else can enter.

~

Today was my bridal shower at Michelle's parents' house in New Jersey. Mom and I went together, while Dad and Nicky were instructed, following the inexplicable and ridiculous tradition of all showers, to come at the end of the party, to say hello, and carry the "loot," as Michelle put it, to the car. As if we poor little girls were too delicate to manage moving a few shopping bags to the driveway. As if the whole party were all about acquiring kitchenware. As if.

For one easy moment, sitting in a big chair in the Donohues' familiar living room, I felt as though I'd come home. I was back in Mendham with my friends from high school and we were girls again, no husbands or boyfriends or fiancés in sight. Only it wasn't the same, because these old friends were chatting with newer ones, friends from college and from work, and we were all adults now, with jobs and plans and secrets. Betsy was there, too, the welcoming diplomat from my new family. Next to her sat my mother, perched on her chair like a bird on a wire, smiling with vague eagerness, a different Jill Beesley from the one who moved away from this town seven years before. As the other mothers confidently joked and chatted, sipping punch and catching up, Betsy leaned her head toward my mother, confiding something I couldn't hear, and my mother looked at her and nodded. Then, as if she knew I was watching, she turned to me and smiled. The smile was full of love, a flash of her old self, and I was grateful she was still well enough to know me and to be with me, that she still knew how to love me. As soon as the moment had passed, I wished, guiltily, that she could give me more, if only for the day, just to make my party like any other bridal shower in any other New Jersey town. This is how I always feel about my mother, full of wincing pride, pulling her toward me and at the same time pushing her away. I want her and I don't want her. I accept what I have—what we have—but it makes me crave more.

~

One of the best things about the shower was that, with the exception of my sorties with Betsy to choose silverware, Nicky has chosen most of the stuff on our registry. This miracle of modern couplehood came about one day after I complained, as usual, that I was doing more of the wedding planning than he was. He told me to give him a job. Fine, I said. Go register for all our kitchen stuff. And before I had a chance to try to influence his decisions, he went out and did it. So when I opened presents at the shower, I was truly surprised and excited by most of the things I got, if those are the right words to describe a reaction to a saucepan or a whisk. As much as I know we'll need all of that stuff, my favorite presents—which I'm sure weren't on Nicky's registry—were the ones that had nothing to do with our upcoming wedding, like a gift certificate for a manicure, a hundred dollar bill, and an adorable pair of earrings.

The worst thing about the shower was the actual date that it took place, which happened to be Nicky's birthday. In my fantastic imagination, I pictured that somehow the shower wouldn't be a big deal, that it wouldn't take over the whole day, but of course it was, and it did. I wish I had known two months ago how nice it would have been for both of us if I had given him a real birthday, something quiet and special that had nothing to do with wedding plans. Instead he got a quick family dinner, a bridal shower rehash, and a book and a shirt from me. Basically, I screwed up, and all my apologies and his almost-easygoing smiles didn't make it right.

(Martha's Vineyard)

Driving to our appointment this afternoon to talk with the minister, Arlene, about the ceremony, Nicky turned to me and asked if I thought we could get married without actually mentioning God. I couldn't believe it. I mean, isn't that like asking a boxer to fight without hitting in the face? I could understand his hesitation about mentioning Jesus, since his father is Jewish, his mother is Episcopalian, and he is none of the above; but ditching God seemed too much to ask. As calmly as I could, I told him that I wished he'd brought up the subject a little sooner, so that we could have talked about it before we were five minutes late to our appointment with the minister. Then I asked if he could maybe think of God in a general, nonreligious way—as a metaphor for nature, for example. He told me he was going to ask Arlene if she could work around God. As if God were some minor character in the Judeo-Christian faith who could be easily edited out. It was so absurd I couldn't argue.

Not that my own feelings about God, and religion in general, are so simple. I was interested in church when I was a kid, and after I'd graduated from Sunday school I became an acolyte, then a lay reader, and even a thurifer once or twice. (This was my favorite job. On certain days of the year, I was responsible for swinging around the censer, a metal contraption which held burning incense, and filling the church with holy smoke.) After high school, I'd pretty much left it behind, except for an occasional Christmas Eve service with my family. After a while I felt like a hypocrite for going to church at all, especially as I learned in college about all the evil things people have done in the name of God. Of course, people have done incredibly good and beautiful things in the name of God as well, and when it came to our wedding, the idea of being married by a minister made sense to me: who else (except maybe for a poet or a musician) would have any idea how to approach bridging the sacred and the profane? At least a spiritual leader has had a lot of practice in talking about love and commitment; it's been part of his or her job description since the beginning of the world.

Now that we're about to get married, and since Mom has become ill, I've started to look at my faith again and ask myself if there might be a place for it in my life after all. My recent experiences in church (singing, praying, bawling my eyes out) have proved that religion still has a hold on me. I like the idea of going, but I'm afraid of the slippery slope: first I'll start going to church every week, and then I'll get roped into joining the choir or the altar guild, and before I know it I'll be one of those Church Ladies, ranting about Satan and video games.

As it turned out, Arlene was perfectly happy to leave out Jesus and God by name. As far as she was concerned, it all flowed from the same source and it didn't matter what you called it. So much for the inflexible institution of religion.

Other than this little adventure, we're all set for the wedding, I think. It feels pretty good to be in the final stretch.

~

The weather has been gorgeous and breezy, and the garden is so beautiful I keep expecting to see fairies and fauns dancing around in it. The best news of all is that in just a few days, my tenure as fiancée will be over forever. Looking back, I realize how vulnerable being engaged has made me feel. I guess because the engagement is all about our intentions, which so far are only words, whereas a wedding is about actually going through with it.

Guests are starting to arrive from both families. My parents are coming tomorrow. Unfortunately, the bridge book project is taking longer than expected, so it will be waiting for me when I get back from our honeymoon. Nicky and I haven't had sex in weeks because we've been so frantic and stressed out. I can't wait for this to start, and I can't wait for it to be over.

Last night I dreamed my hair was long and beautiful. Why the hell did I cut it all off? I suppose it was my final act of rebellion against the wedding rule books, which always say that a newly engaged woman should let her hair grow—but it's left me looking in the mirror and wondering who I am. I am a boy. No, a girl. Make that woman.

Get it over with already; make me a wife.

PART
TWO

The Newlyweds

As September approached, the nice, easygoing me began to mutate into a monstrous cartoon of a stressed-out, over-emotional bride-to-be. Night after night I found myself awake at 4:00 A.M. convinced that I had overpaid the caterer or underpacked for the honeymoon. Instead of doing the things that always made me feel better, like writing in my journal or taking long walks, I entangled myself in decisions I shouldn't have been trying to make, such as how many bottles of tonic we'd need for the bar, or whether the band would prefer to drink wine or beer (as if there could be any debate: do rowdy, electrified six-man bands sip Chardonnay?). The fact that I was about to make an irrevocable promise to spend the rest of my life with Nicky was entirely subsumed by the meticulous planning of the wedding. At the time I was only dimly aware that there were really two separate events about to take place: the one, a simple ceremony in which Nicky and I would sign a marriage license and say our vows; and the other, the biggest party anyone in either family had ever put together. And the party was winning. This was going to be a gala wedding, complete with a breathtaking setting, beautiful flowers, and a funky wedding gown made just for me. The only problem was that the more involved I became with planning my dream wedding, the more guilty I felt about actually getting what I wanted.

The money I spent on my wedding dress, I reminded myself, could have paid our rent for a month. The "deluxe" Porta-Johns, with mirrors and running water (which I insisted were preferable to the old-fashioned construction-site models), would have paid off two months' worth of my student loan. I was torn between wanting the Stuff—the perfect wedding, the most delicious food, the shiniest diamond ring—and feeling ashamed of wanting it. It was a classic conflict of values, an attempt to assert my own style over that which I perceived to be my family's. Although my father was unfailingly generous and supportive when it came to helping with the wedding, I knew that this spectacular event was something that neither he nor my mother would ever have dreamed of doing for themselves, and I still wasn't sure that my new "style" was anything to be proud of.

Despite these nagging questions, I pressed on with arranging and rearranging things as planned. And as I pondered whether I had become a materialistic narcissist, I was interrupted by a further philosophical query that kept repeating itself in my mind: what girl in her right mind goes down the aisle without having her hair and makeup done by a professional? Upon the recommendation of a friend, I called a hair and makeup stylist named Brigitte and booked her to come to our house on the morning of the wedding to do my mother's hair, then Auntie Sylvia's, before turning me into a vision of bridal beauty. She asked me to come to her salon the day before the wedding so we could do a test run, called a "prebridal." It's kind of like prepping for surgery. I showed up at her salon on Friday morning, twenty-eight hours before I was supposed to get married. Brigitte sat me down in a chair and looked me over.

"Your eyebrows need shaping," she said. "And these blemishes . . ." She ran a finger across my forehead, frowning. She called over her daughter, Robin, who surveyed me with equal concern. Brigitte turned to her. "Can we get her a facial?" she asked. "Look at her eyebrows. Can Trish do a wax?"

I don't think much of facials, but I was putty in their hands. Luckily, Robin informed Brigitte that there were absolutely no appointments available. The women started toward the front desk, conferring quietly. Brigitte glanced back at me. I heard her say something about home treatment. They disappeared around the corner. A few minutes later, she returned with a bulging plastic bag. "I'm going to do your eyebrows myself," she said. "And as for your skin, tonight I want you to wash your face with this." She pulled a bottle out of the bag and dropped it in my lap. "Then apply this mask in a very thin layer across your forehead." She handed me a tube. "After ten minutes, rinse it off and then apply this toner with a cotton ball." Another bottle. "Then apply the moisturizer, but not on your forehead. Only where you're dry."

The bill for the products alone was $120, and I knew that there was no cream on earth that could change my skin overnight; but at that point I would have had my front teeth removed if Brigitte had told me to. She washed my hair, dried it with a round brush, and set it with hot rollers. She plucked my eyebrows and rubbed toner on my face. She left me for fifteen minutes. When she removed the rollers, we both realized that there had been a terrible mistake. My hair was so curly it had formed a puffy, cata-strophic halo around my head. Brigitte tried everything to batten it down, but nothing worked. The mood at the salon was grim.

"It was just an experiment," she assured me. "Tomor-row I'll skip the rollers. Don't worry."

In the course of the eight months leading up to this day, it had never occurred to me that I might actually look ugly at my wedding. All brides look good at their wed-dings; it's one of the few bonuses that nature hands out in life, in the same category as postflu weight loss and a midpregnancy glow. Sitting in the chair, with my hair scraping the ceiling and my brow red from plucking, I suddenly wondered if, in some miraculous upset of the natural order of things, I was going to end up looking like Little Orphan Annie.

That night I stayed with my family at the house they were renting a few doors down from Nicky's family's house. Before my parents arrived on the island, I had gone to the store and bought the things I knew they would want to eat: oatmeal, eggs, tea, 2 percent milk, apples, cheddar cheese, and a package of chocolate chip cookies. When I got to the house, they were drinking the tea and eating the cookies. A few of the apples were gone. I felt keenly aware of being their daughter, a grown daughter, wanting to protect them and help them as much as I could. I also realized how much my own shopping list had diverged from theirs since I'd grown up. But I could still shop for them—it didn't mean I had stopped belonging to them, or them to me.

The next morning I scrubbed my face and used the clay mask. My forehead looked clear to me. The wedding was not until four, so I went for a walk to the beach with my family: Mom, Dad, Tony, Sabina, Gordon, and Jessie. I was surprised at how calm I felt. At one, Brigitte arrived to begin working her dangerous hair magic. She was not carrying rollers. Tony was outside in a lawn chair with a notepad, composing his toast, as his wife, Sabina, gave him pointers. My younger brother, Gordon, was snoozing on the couch next to Jessie, his girlfriend. I was tying ribbons onto chocolate lollipops to give away as favors while Mom kept me company. Everything seemed to be under control.

And just like that it was almost four. The photographer, who had documented everyone getting ready, went ahead with my parents to join Nicky's family at their house. Just as my bridesmaids and I were about to leave for the ceremony, the phone rang: it was my mother's cousin from England, who was stranded at her nearby inn without a ride. After fifteen minutes of back-and-forth calls, we arranged to get her a lift. Again we gathered up to leave, and again the phone rang: it was the flower girl's mother, saying that little Julie was too scared to walk down the aisle alone. We decided to have her older sister walk with her down the aisle. Finally we were off, a half-hour behind schedule, walking the short distance to the house where the event would begin. Our starting the ceremony late caused a chain reaction which meant that the ceremony musicians, hired for only an hour, had to disappear halfway through to perform at another wedding ceremony. I learned later—I'm not kidding—that they were replaced by a one-armed electric piano player named Joe. But other than that, things went smoothly. Dan and Erin sang a hymn in Latin from the back of the congregation; Sonya recited a poem she'd memorized in our honor; Nicky and

I said our vows in front of a flower-covered trellis under a blue sky; and finally, Arlene turned to me, as we had planned, and said, "Amanda, you may kiss the *groom*." Everyone laughed and clapped, and we walked down the aisle, holding hands, married at last.

Throughout the reception, I worried about everything, from my failing to personally greet everyone to whether our cocktail hour was dragging on for too long. There were moments when I felt something like loneliness, feeling somehow unapproachable in my conspicuous dress and celebrated position. People were treating me differently, and I didn't know how to act. Across the lawn, Nicky had his hands full with two guests who had apparently been left off the seating chart. There were many blunders, like my stepping on my veil and ripping it off my head as Nicky dipped me during our first dance, and an excited guest pouring a beer all over Nicky's shirt; and there were wonderful moments, like when my friend Matthew caught the bouquet and gave his boyfriend Will a huge Hollywood kiss. My parents danced all night long, and when I emerged from the whirlwind long enough to notice, I saw Mom dancing with Nicky's father, Elliot dancing with Sue, Auntie Sylvia and Brenda dancing with Paul, and Karen doing the jitterbug with Luke. I should add that our cake-cutting ceremony was as quiet as can be, and no one ended up with a face full of butter cream.

What I'll remember best is how it felt when Nicky and

I stood before Arlene and said our vows. The rest of the world disappeared—gone were our families and our friends and the perfect garden and the geese flying overhead and the one-armed electric piano player—and all that was left was the two of us. I was falling into Nicky's blue eyes, and he was holding my hands, and we were saying yes to each other. Yes. At that moment nothing mattered except for Nicky, and it seemed as though we could float away together on the ocean breeze if that's what we wanted. Anything was possible.

By the time we left the reception, I was more exhausted than I'd ever been in my life. We drove to our room—called the "bridal suite," although I wasn't sure why—and spread out the picnic Nicky's mother had put together for us. We were suddenly starving, and we ate everything in sight, drank some champagne, and looked at each other expectantly. It was 11:30 P.M. The room was devoid of telephone, television, books, and games. There was nothing to do in that room except to make love and then sleep. Maybe that's what made it a bridal suite. Tara and David were wrong about this one: I didn't cry once during the wedding, and I can state with confidence that Nicky wasn't wishing he could be partying with his friends instead of being in bed with me.

Looking back, I don't think I could say it was the best day of my life. For me it was a *huge* day, an exciting and unsettling and thrilling event—but too unique to be ranked on a scale among all the other days of working and eating and walking the dog. No, that day came twenty-four hours after that. The happiest I'd felt for a long time was on the flight to Italy, en route to our trans-European honeymoon. Suddenly we were ourselves again, only better somehow. Nicky and I drank champagne, cuddled under our Lufthansa blankets, and congratulated ourselves for pulling it all off. We had a honeymoon to go on, and then the rest of our lives would begin.

SEPTEMBER

(Paganico, Italy)

We've spent the past few nights just outside this tiny Tuscan village, about halfway between Rome and Florence near the western coast of Italy. I've loved watching and listening to Nicky speak Italian, although all his language skills could not get us a break at the rental car company when the lady at the desk pointed out that his license was expired. Really, couldn't he have seen that one coming? Luckily his thinking-ahead bride had both a current license and credit card just in case.

By day we've been cooking pasta, drinking red wine produced on the property, reading, and daydreaming about moving to Italy for a year. By night I dream that we need money and are somehow involved in a shady business deal with a sexy Italian movie star who then morphs into Torey, the champion dodgeball player from my grade school gym class.

We drive from here to the southern coast of France tomorrow. I'm ready to move on, believe it or not, as much as I've enjoyed all the peace and simplicity of our little villa in the hills of Tuscany. So much for living here. Enough grasshoppers and long siestas from twelve-thirty to four; I'm ready for some action. After the tumult of the wedding, I feel restless with nothing to do but read. (Yesterday I finished the complete works of Oscar Wilde and have started *Moby-Dick*, which I've discovered will be a really good book to pick up if I'm ever having trouble sleeping.)

~

(Antibes, France)

What is it about French beaches that wherever I decide to put my towel, I invariably end up next to a beautiful, tanned, topless supermodel? And why do I then have to point her out to Nicky and then hope for some kind of negative (or at best neutral) response from him upon seeing her? (Fake boobs did nothing to mitigate how attractive this particular woman was.) Nicky does not, as a rule, look at other women when he's with me—but when you're on the Riviera, what else can you do? We were both checking out everyone who walked by.

There was a lunar eclipse last night, and we sat on the balcony of our hotel room and watched the moon dissolve into a sliver. It was magical and strange, just like our trip so far. The best part of being on honeymoon is the feeling that from now on, we can do whatever we wish with our lives together. And so we daydream about moving to every place we visit, but especially here, where a small and fluffy

Yorkshire terrier like Emma would be welcome at all the best tables.

Tomorrow the Picasso museum and then the train up to Paris for our last two nights. Then it's back home to pick up Emma and return to our lives in New York. Our apartment seems so far away.

(Paris, France)

First time in Paris since I came here for a semester during my junior year of college nine years ago. It looks different to me: there's a McDonald's in place of the café where I used to go for my *croque monsieur*, and there's a Häagen-Dazs shop where my favorite movie theater used to be. Being here now reminds me of how much I've changed since I was twenty. I used to wear black skirts and smoke Gauloises and write in my journal while sipping a *café simple*. Everywhere I went I met new people—at the Shakespeare bookstore (now totally renovated after a fire some years ago), in classes at l'Université, sitting in the Luxembourg gardens. I felt like I belonged; or at least I felt as if I had earned my right to exist there as a stranger.

Now I'm here as an almost-thirty-year-old married lady from America. I feel like an ordinary tourist, buying expensive underwear from a trendy shop in the Marais, looking at pictures in the Musée D'Orsay, walking with my husband along the Seine. It's not so bad, I suppose. At least on this visit I can afford a real dinner instead of making spaghetti on a hot plate, as I did when I was here as a student. I can't believe I cooked my dinners in the bathroom for ten months of my life. I can't believe I let a Frenchman I'd just met drive me around Paris on his scooter. I can't believe how short I wore my skirts. And, at other moments, I can't believe I'll never do those things again.

Some things haven't changed at all. We went to a men's store and looked at a few dress shirts for Nicky. He chose one he liked, unfolded and unpinned it to hold up in front of the mirror, and a crazed saleslady spun in like the Tasmanian Devil and started screaming at him for messing with the shirts. We summoned all of our combined memory of the French language and told her she was a monster (*monstreuse*) and impolite (*impolite*). Such is the extent of our vocabulary. I should have called her a *fiancée*.

Last night, after a wonderful dinner (Grand Marnier soufflé for dessert), we walked for two hours all over the city, trying to recall the places where we'd been and when. We came across the apartment building where I used to rent a room, and there outside the door was the same old man who sold crêpes to me when I lived there. As it turned out, Nicky used to go to the same guy when he spent a month in Paris five years ago. The man was happy enough to sell us crêpes smeared with Nutella, but he certainly didn't remember either of us. No matter—at that moment it seemed to us that not only did we have a future together, we had something of a past as well.

~

(Back Home)

And married. Welcoming us back to the apartment were a pile of bills, a zillion phone calls to return, and more edits to do on the stupid bridge book. Thud. We received a few wedding gifts while we were gone, so there will be thank-you notes to write as well. I don't mind writing them once I sit down and start, but they always take so damned long. This is because I want to say something original in each one: to be a real writer, I suppose. A real wife. So far Nicky and I have been splitting the thank-you-note task down the middle, more or less. He has yet to attack his list, and so I find myself nagging him to get them done. I don't want to be a carping wife, but I'm also aware that his response (or lack thereof) to the gifts reflects on both of us now. It doesn't seem right that I should write all the thank-you notes just because I know it's important. He needs to realize it's important, too. I'm working on him.

It's been hard to readjust to the city. I haven't seen any of my friends yet, and I've barely talked to them on the phone. They seem distant to me—as if they're standing a step back to wait for me to settle into marriage or something. Or maybe it's me who is standing back. I suppose these are postwedding blues: no more attention or excitement. Couples who have just gotten married are much less interesting than ones who are just about to. All of our optimism is now silently, unglamorously put to the test.

And then there's the name issue. I've kept mine, because I like it, and because I've begun my writing career under this name, and because I don't see why I *should* change it, any more than Nicky should change his. I understand the appeal of us having one name, of being united as a family, but the problem is that someone's got to make a sacrifice to make it happen. We both offered, half-heartedly, to take the other's name, but it didn't seem fair either way. Then we thought about combining names—not with an awkward hyphen, but making one name out of two. "Weinsley" didn't quite work, and Nicky rejected "Beestock" as too cartoony. (Nevertheless, Julia has adopted this as our new name, and now all correspondence and phone calls from her begin, "Hi, Beestock!") I decided to remain a Beesley, and we agreed that if we have kids, we'll give them Nicky's last name—if only because motherhood is indisputable enough not to have to be named. Oddly, I've noticed that people don't really listen when you tell them you're keeping your name. Even my father, who has been both roughly and gently schooled in feminism since I started my freshman year at Barnard, addressed his first letter to me as "Mrs. Nicholas Weinstock." I called him immediately and explained that *keeping* my name meant that I wasn't *changing* it. I think he gets it. But Jeez.

One more thing: what's with everyone asking, "How's married life?" as if I just sprang from Nicky's forehead? Married life is a hell of a lot like the unmarried life I've lived for the past few years. Only now I have a husband.

~

Yesterday was my thirtieth birthday, which I knew would be a quiet affair, coming on the heels of our wedding and honeymoon. Nicky gave me a set of books that I'd mentioned I wanted to read some day, Proust's *Remembrance of Things Past*. A nice present, to be sure, only the thing was I already had the exact same set in our bookshelves at home. They'd been there since we moved in together, but I guess he never noticed. The whole thing was a bummer: I didn't tell him right away because I didn't want him to feel bad, but then I thought he'd feel dumb if he ever noticed the other set. Finally I blurted it out, and we both got to be miserable for a few hours.

Having my own birthday fall flat reminded me that Nicky's had been no carnival either, and I realized how important it will be to pay attention to these things in the future. Now that we're husband and wife—each other's main support staff and cheerleader—we'd better not forget to pick up the pom-poms when the occasion calls for it.

I'm not sure whether I'd call this postwedding blues or a newlywed tiff. Either way, it's dull and annoying. With the all-consuming ceremony now reduced to an engraved leather album full of photos, life seems to have flattened as well. I'm almost done with the stupid bridge book, and besides a permanent dislike for card games, this has left me looking forward, worriedly, to my next professional prospect. My play appears to be a nonstarter. Writing short stories is no way to make a living. A writer is the dumbest thing I could want to be—and, as it turns out, the only thing I want to be.

These, inarguably, are *not* the best days of my life.

OCTOBER

Just got a call from Judy, the editor from *Self* I met with last March. She said she saw our wedding announcement in the *Times* and remembered liking my writing, and she wanted to know if I would be interested in auditioning to write a column about the first year of my marriage. As if I'd say no. I whipped off a couple of sample columns and sent them to her within a few days. I am up against two other people, so I wanted my columns to get there first. I really want this job (it's got to be better than endlessly typing up the requirements for a no-trump bid), but I'm trying not to get my hopes up.

~

I dreamed last night that I was sitting with a little girl in the middle of a fenced-in garden. She was someone I had known when I was a kid, but we had grown apart over the years. It was odd, because while I had become an adult, she had remained a child. She told me that her mother had just died. I started crying. When the tears finally subsided, it seemed as though we had somehow come to a truce, and that from then on we would be friends. When I woke up I was sure that the girl in the dream was actually me. More than that, she was saying out loud the one thing I couldn't say, and feared most, about my mother: that she was already gone.

I guess we all disappear as we grow: I'm not the same as I was when I was a child, just as Mom isn't the same as she was five years ago. There are parts of our personalities, our souls, even, that will never come back. Of course it's different for Mom. She still has her spirit, the merry kindness that informs everything she does, but there was an old Mom and now there's a new one. And as much as I love this new mother, I miss the old one, the woman who could guide a group of twelve on a ten-mile hike, who knew when to leave the path and bushwhack to a perfect blueberry-picking spot, or a sunny vista, or a private swimming pond.

I wonder what happens to a person's soul when dementia sets in. Does it stay trapped inside the body? I hope it takes off on little day trips, flying away to somewhere beautiful and coming back every once in a while to rest.

~

Things I've noticed since turning thirty:

1. There are now too many gray hairs on my head to pluck them all out.
2. I've stopped making biological clock jokes.
3. I'm good at Trivial Pursuit simply because I've been around so long.
4. Every day the newspaper features an article about some twenty-year-old who sold his dumb Web site for tens of millions of dollars.
5. People who were born the same year I started high school are already in *college*.

~

Nicky is giving a final push toward finishing his first novel, a book he's been working on since before he met me. I have my fingers crossed that he finishes it soon and sells it quickly. It means so much to him, and he's one of those people who always triumphs when he tries something. If it didn't work out, I think he would take it hard—especially now that we're married. I know that he now feels more strongly than ever that he has to earn a lot of money and be as successful as possible in order to prove himself a good husband. And somewhere deep down, I hope he can. Not because I want him to take care of me, but because I know he won't be happy with himself otherwise.

I have finally completed my work on the bloody bridge book. By the end of our collaboration, the Guru wanted to kill me for not loving the game as much as he does. Truth is, no matter how desperate I was for the work, I just couldn't get excited about spotting a ruff in the dummy. Sue me.

We leave for New Hampshire tomorrow for a visit to my parents. I'm looking forward to some time in the country—lately city life has seemed difficult in the most ridiculous ways. Just going out for the newspaper yesterday, I had to step over several piles of garbage, duck as two mad four-year-olds doused the area with power water pistols, and witness a screaming match between two fat men over a parking space.

~

(New Hampshire)

The drive up here was amazing; all the trees have trotted out their colors before they go to sleep for the winter. The air smells good, too. We got to my parents' house at three, had tea and cookies, went for a walk, and then it was time to start making dinner. The menu: salmon, brussels sprouts, baked potatoes, salad, and, as usual, apple crumble.

We used to eat apple crumble twice a week when I was a kid. Mom could whip one off in fifteen minutes. She'd peel the apples, slicing them into the square Pyrex dish she always used, and then sprinkle the fruit with lemon juice, sugar, and cinnamon. In another bowl she would mix together oats, brown sugar, flour, and chopped walnuts, measuring each ingredient with a cupped hand. Then, using her fingers, she'd work a half stick of butter into the flour mixture, finally pressing it on top of the apples with her floury hands. The top of the crumble would always have the impression of her fingers where she patted it down. She would put the crumble in the oven and let it cook while we ate dinner. I must have seen her do it a hundred times.

Tonight I realized that she can't do it anymore. We were all pitching in to make the dinner: Dad was making a salad, Nicky was scrubbing the potatoes, and Mom and I were in charge of dessert. I got out a bag of apples and a couple of paring knives, and we started peeling. Mom got halfway through one apple, put it down by the stove, and picked up a new one. I was working next to her, peeling the apples and slicing them into a big bowl. She peeled a second apple, dropping bits of peel and stem into the bowl I was using for the clean sliced apples and leaving the slices on the counter. I rescued the original half-peeled apple from beside the stove and finished slicing it. She dropped another handful of peels into the bowl of apple slices. As I separated the peels from the apples, she turned her attention to the crumble. She picked up the mixing bowl, hesitating, looking at me but then looking away.

The flour was in its usual tin on the counter, and the sugar was right in front of her. I wanted to help, thought about handing her a measuring cup and reminding her how to start, but I had a feeling that it would embarrass her and make things worse. She reached for a fork, and with her other hand picked up a dish towel. She stood there for a minute, her eyes filling with tears, and then, barely loud enough for me to hear, she said, "I used to make them all the time."

It was the first time I'd ever heard her refer to the way she used to be. She dropped the fork and hurried into the bedroom, crying, the dish towel clutched in her hand. My father followed her, and Nicky and I were left alone in the kitchen. I started mixing together the flour and sugar mixture, concentrating on it as if it were some secret formula that would save the world. Nicky watched as I finished the thing and stuck it in the oven. He came over and put his arms around me, and I felt a wave of remorse. "I should have helped her more," I said. "I should have given her an easier job." Nicky replied, "You didn't do anything wrong. I swear you didn't do anything wrong."

Ten minutes later my parents came back out, my mother cheerful again, the whole incident forgotten, at least by her. Nicky put on an Elton John record that he knows she loves, and as we finished setting the table we all sang along to "Crocodile Rock."

One of the things I've always said to make myself feel better about this dementia—or Alzheimer's, or whatever it is that nobody seems to be able to do anything about—is that at least my mother is happy. And for the most part, she is. She's usually cheerful and engaged by the world, with a childlike interest in nature and people. But tonight I was reminded that she's not happy all the time, and that she is no more protected from the knowledge of what's happening to her than we are. I don't know if this realization sticks, if she remembers that she is ill, or if every time she realizes she's not the way she used to be it comes as a fresh terror.

How do I look at my mother and not see my own future? This disease runs in the family: my father told me recently that Mom's father, my granddad, had suffered from something similar, although it was undiagnosed at the time. Mom and I are alike in many ways, and people who see us together have always been able to tell that we were mother and daughter. I have her smile, her gait, her height. I can only hope, guiltily, that the inheritance ends there. Knowing that my father's side of the family is not prone to Alzheimer's or dementia, I'm constantly comparing myself to both sides of the family: do I have my mother's legs or my father's hair? My mother's skin or my father's eyes? And whose brain do I have, the one that chugs on until it's eighty-six, or the one that starts to fail at fifty-five?

~

Nicky and my father are a good team. This afternoon they spent two hours fixing the window on our car door. My dad is one of those handyman types who would rather build it or fix it than buy it or send it to the shop. Nicky has that side of him as well, and so he loves to work with my dad when he comes to visit. They always have some kind of project going on. I walked by the garage today and saw them working side by side without speaking. I'm always interested in the silent communion of men at work. I know if I were in the same spot with Nicky's mom, we'd be chatting away.

I guess that old saying about marrying your father is true, at least in part. Nicky is very different from my father—in all the ways an engineer and a writer are, by nature, different—but still he has the same essential loyalty and sense of responsibility that my father has. This is good for me, especially if I do end up with Alzheimer's in thirty years. I know that Nicky will take care of me the way that my father takes care of my mother.

~

Exhausted from a climb to the top of Smart's Mountain with Nicky, Mom, and Dad. My parents are in better shape than I am. I think they like walking in the woods more than anything, a fact about them that hasn't changed for as long as I can remember.

I realize that if I read the previous paragraph, say, in twenty years, I'll take it as absolute fact. But memory is so slippery. What if I accidentally wrote the date incorrectly? Or what if I misheard the name of the mountain and it was really Smith's, not Smart's? How impressive it is that anyone can remember anything: a recipe for apple crumble, or the directions to New York City, or even the date of a wedding.

This comes home to me when people kindly ask how long my mother has been ill. I never know the answer. I remember coming home from high school one day and finding that she had put her purse in the bread box. If it happened now, I would consider it a typical manifestation of dementia, but at the time she did it she was getting straight A's in college. (While I was in high school, Mom commuted from Mendham to Rutgers every day and got her degree in chemistry and nutrition.) Then there was the Christmas five years ago when she forgot to put Gordon's present under the tree (it was his main present—a camera), but maybe that was because she was too caught up in organizing and cooking for a holiday party at our house the next day. For that matter, why couldn't my father have remembered it? We expect mothers to do so much, and my mother did it all, from driving me to softball to taking Tony fishing to finding Gordon a drumming teacher. On top of that, she earned her B.S., joined the volunteer ambulance squad in our town, won gold medals in amateur ski races, and organized group hiking trips. Come to think of it, she was more of a feminist than most of my professors at Barnard, although she would never have put it that way. She was a wife, a mother, a student, a community organizer, an athlete, and a volunteer. Who wouldn't forget a few things with all that she was doing?

Over time, however, the forgetting turned frightening. The change has been slow and creeping, like vines growing around and then over the windows of a house. It was only with the so-called "diagnosis" that I've been convinced that it hasn't all been a misunderstanding, that she isn't going to wake up one morning, say, "I feel better now," and start her life again.

~

After dinner I showed my parents our album of wedding pictures. We were sitting on the sofa in front of the TV, which happened to be showing a program that involved a wedding. My mother had trouble separating the wedding on the television from the wedding in the pictures—making comments about us to the screen, and vice versa—and I found myself getting angry. I realized that I wanted her to dwell lovingly on every picture, to take one and have it framed for the mantel, to send out copies to all her friends. So many demands! I know they're not reasonable; even if her memory were intact they would not be. But I can't help wanting it. At times like this I'm afraid of becoming a mother myself. I'm scared of having those same demands—or different ones—placed on me and being unable to fulfill them.

~

(Back Home)

I got the job at *Self*! They're going to use one of my audition columns as the first in the series, and after that I'll be writing a one-page essay each month, complete with glossy photo, about how our marriage is doing. I know too much about this business to think this is a *big* break, but I do know it's *a* break. At least now if someone wants to see something I've written, I'll have more to show than just a diagram of a bridge hand.

When Judy called me to tell me I'd been chosen for the job, my first panicked thought was that I would be expected to write about *everything*. I'm not scared of writing about Nicky and me—I think it will be an interesting experiment to publicly document our first year together—but I can't imagine writing anything about my mother. And so I won't. The job is to write about my marriage, not my whole life. And although Mom is often on my mind, I do have days and even weeks when I'm too caught up in my own life with Nicky, and in my own successes and disappointments, to spend too much time thinking about her.

My second thought, upon hearing the news, is that I am finally an equal partner in this marriage of two writers. It makes me feel powerful to have landed a great writing job without any help, to be bringing in money, and to be on track for the future. When people ask me what I do, at last I'll have an answer that makes sense to me when I say it. I'm proud of myself. Nicky, meanwhile, is calling everyone he knows to tell them the news. Probably just trying to get in my good graces so I don't publish a column that makes him look like a jerk.

~

Betsy went into the hospital for a hip replacement operation she'd been planning for a long time. We visited her today. When I walked into the room, I was frightened to see her in a hospital bed, looking so vulnerable. She was the other mother in my life, and I didn't want anything to happen to her. Nicky, too, was doting and protective. But the doctor who performed the surgery came in and told her she was in great shape. He promised she'd be out and about again in a few weeks. Knowing Betsy, she'll cut that time in half, and by the end of a month will be jogging in the park again.

I have to admit, guiltily, that it was something of a relief to see that someone else's physically fit and competent mom is not, in fact, indestructible. That I wasn't the only child forced to mother a mother. But with that relief came the return of a large and paralyzing fear. Is any of us safe from the secret crumbling of our bodies? And when the dust—and the marriage, and the career—finally settles, will there be any mothers left for me to love?

$$\sim$$

Went to dinner with Sonya and Karen, which turned out to be a good, old-fashioned girls' night, complete with gossip, red wine, cigarettes, and fancy desserts, all of which I needed more than I knew. I had been feeling a bit hurt over not hearing much from either of them since getting back from our honeymoon (totally unfair of me, I know, since I wasn't exactly burning up the telephone lines to get through to them either), so it was a relief to be back in touch. I realize that I'm still adjusting to this newlywed thing, wondering whether I am different or am just being perceived differently, and paranoid that my friends will assume I don't need them anymore. Or won't need me.

Being with Karen and Sonya again made me feel that everything was back to normal. At the same time, I was keenly aware of being the only married woman at the table. I noticed it most when they were talking about their boyfriends. Usually we're all pretty open with each other about the ups and downs of our various relationships, but after Karen told us about problems she'd been having with Mark, and Sonya chimed in about an argument she'd had with Doug, I just nodded in empathy. I didn't feel like talking about Nicky, even though I could easily have come up with things to say.

For example, his daily routine, which I found so charming and admirable for the first few years of knowing him, has started to bug me. In fact, it has taken on a sinister life of its own. Every single morning it's the same thing: sit-ups, coffee, e-mail, Nutri-Grain bar, orange juice, writing. And after he's worked for five hours, then it's off to the gym, where I'm sure he does the same exercises, chatting with no one, wasting no time. What is it with men? Why are they so tied to their rituals? And what can it possibly mean for me but a future of worn-down shoes, uninteresting breakfasts, and the early morning racket of coffee beans in the grinder? That night, as I was leaving to meet my friends, I went into Nicky's office, deliberately eating a Nutri-Grain bar in the early evening, just to see what he would do. He pretended not to notice—but his face registered panic as he realized that I might be eating the last bar, and then relief as he remembered, correctly, that there was still one left in the box. Mission partially accomplished. I had rattled—if not brought down—the system.

I know I could have complained about Nicky to my friends. Sonya would have rolled her eyes and said, "He may be predictable, but at least he's got a flat stomach." Or Karen would have topped my gripes with a tale of Mark's obsessive ironing of his T-shirts. On the way home from the restaurant, I wondered if they noticed my silence, whether they thought that marriage had made me dull and complacent—or worse, that my silence might be perceived as superiority. The last thing I felt was superior. It's not as though I thought they wouldn't understand; after all, such complaints had been the fodder for all our late-night grumblings in the past. The thing was, it felt ungrateful to complain about Nicky after they'd had to listen to me talk about the wedding for nine months, schlep all the way to Massachusetts for the ceremony, and then pore over the wedding pictures a dozen times once it was over.

I was being dumb. The people who came to our wedding promised to help me and Nicky uphold our promises to each other, and who better to do this than my best friends? More than anyone else, these two women know me. They're smart. If I say that Nicky's bugging me, they're not going to lower their heads toward each other as soon as I leave for the bathroom and whisper, "I *knew* he wasn't right for her." But I remember how I felt when Michelle got married, as if I'd suddenly been left behind, and it makes me wonder if my single friends feel that way now. If they do, it won't help to talk on endlessly about Nicky. At the same time, it might hurt to hold back from them.

I can't tell exactly what's so different about being married; I only know that things seem weightier now that they're tied to a whole life. Everything that happens sets a precedent. The first married gift flop. The first married argument over laundry. The first married evening of choosing TV over sex, or choosing to visit his parents before my parents, or staying home rather than going to a party. There are nice firsts, too, like getting ready to fill out the customs forms on the plane ride back from our honeymoon and realizing that we only needed one. Now that we share one life, so to speak, it's time to start building that life. Starting from scratch.

NOVEMBER

Mom's sixtieth birthday today. My brothers and I sent her a big bunch of flowers, which we figured would be a festive and visible reminder that it was a special day, because otherwise she might not remember. Before I knew what this illness was, I would go out and buy her things to encourage a hobby or some kind of independent activity—

a book about horses that would miraculously rekindle her childhood love of riding, or a box of charcoal pencils that would get her started sketching again. It was my attempt to make her better, to get her interested in something that would change her life. Now I figure that the charcoal pencils and the horse book would be put away and forgotten, but the flowers will cheer her up every day—at least for a week.

Not that she has ever been picky about presents. No matter what we kids gave Mom for her birthday or Christmas, she was always happy with it. Her mother, my gran, was the opposite. When I was a kid, we'd go visit her in England every two or three years, and whenever Mom gave her a present, Gran would always give it back and tell my mother she didn't need it, that she should keep it herself. It drove my mother crazy. Gran would bustle around all day long, washing socks and cooking things she remembered we kids liked. She'd be so busy taking care of all of us that she wouldn't let herself relax. Mom would feel bad that Gran was working so hard and probably felt guilty about it, too. It was always a fight to get Gran to sit down with us and eat. I know that she and my mother loved each other, but they didn't seem to know how to deal with each other. I'd like to know more about their relationship, especially when Mom was growing up. Was *her* mother helpful and excited when it came time for *her* wedding? But she doesn't remember much about her childhood these days. Her closest living relative is her only sister in England, so the stories of my mother's childhood can't be passed down to me easily. But even if Auntie Sylvia had been living down the street for the past ten years, I probably wouldn't have asked many questions. I'd always felt it a betrayal to ask others about my mother, as if it was an admission that my mother would be unable to tell me herself.

It's only now that stories are out of my reach that I want so desperately to hear them. So I collect whatever truth I can find and make up the rest.

~

Nicky and I went to the country to look for a new place to live, and we may have just found the perfect house. It feels strange to be writing this, since we've both always loved the city so much, but lately the idea of moving has become more compelling.

It started just over a year ago, when the city began maintenance work on the water pipes running under our street. Starting every morning at seven, a truckload of workers would arrive with pavement-crushing machines and begin tearing up big chunks of concrete in front of our building. To call it loud doesn't do it justice: it was an earthquake, and we were at the epicenter. People who live in cities soon adjust to new noises, especially people in our part of Manhattan, which is never without the boisterous yells of bar-hopping college kids, the thwomping beat as cars roll by with stereos blasting salsa music from full-sized speakers, and the thunderclap every morning at three when the restaurant across the street slams down its security gate. But this was different; when the cacophony came to a lunch-break lull at noon, and we could finally make a phone call without hiding in the closet to be heard, the normally grating sounds of the ice cream truck jingle and band practice in the basement next door sounded like birds tweeting. We were determined to get used to this new challenge, of course, just as we'd gotten used to everything difficult about living in New York City.

Around the same time, I went into Nicky's office and saw he had cut out a picture from *The New York Times* and tacked it to the bulletin board over his desk. It showed a man, a fishing pole in hand, sitting on a rock in front of a perfectly still lake at sunrise. The caption said, "A fisherman tries his luck in Putnam County." Over the next six months, the picture began to represent an escape from everything crazy in New York City. When the loony woman across the street screamed out the window for hours in a language neither of us recognized, we'd say, "This kind of thing would never happen in Putnam County." When our rent went up after the first year, we wondered about the size of the farmhouse we could find for the same rent in Putnam County. We pictured each having our own office, with windows that looked out at trees instead of brick walls, and we daydreamed about letting Emma out to play without having to walk six blocks for the nearest patch of grass. Eventually we began to start our sentences with, "When we get to Putnam County . . ." It made sense to live somewhere beautiful and quiet. As writers, we had the kind of job that would let us go anywhere. Why not take to the hills?

This is how Nicky and I make decisions together: he comes up with an idea, somewhat dreamy, often wishful, always creative, and I talk and plan and hammer out the details. He's the architect, I guess, and I'm the builder. This pattern holds true for much of what we do, from getting engaged to painting the bedroom a new color. The roles are always reversible, but they're roles nonetheless.

Once we got married, I suggested that we at least *visit* this famous Putnam County, after talking about it for so long. The first few trips were largely unsuccessful—rainy days of wandering through lonely small towns, trying to picture ourselves fitting in. We decided to give it one more try, this time with a real estate broker. Which brings us to today.

We met the broker in Garrison, a little town about forty miles north of the city on the Hudson River. First we looked at a couple of apartments in town—stuffy, wall-to-wall-carpeted affairs that didn't come close to fitting our ideal of a quiet place in the country. The broker said she had one more place to show us, a house that belonged to an old friend. She drove us down one dirt road and off that one onto another, and as we turned the corner, we saw the house: a charming yellow cottage that used to house farmhands. We were met at the door by the young couple who were currently living there: he was a jazz musician and she worked for a not-for-profit organization. They were moving because they'd just bought a place about a mile away, and promised to have us over for a barbecue as soon as we moved.

Nicky and I fell in love with the house right away. It was warm and cozy, gently creaky, beautifully quiet. The trees were changing colors and the mountains in the distance were purple. The front porch looked out over a field of grazing horses. The landlords had a pool we could use, and there were hiking trails nearby. The rent was cheaper than what we were paying for our noisy, cramped apartment. As we left, we offered to put down a deposit but the broker said we didn't have to bother. We could have the place if we wanted it, she said. We just had to let her know within a week. So we told her we'd talk it over. Husbands and wives do that, you know. They talk things over. They live in houses, trimming their lawns and hobnobbing with neighbors.

Looks like we will, too.

~

I feel scared and excited even thinking about moving, especially after living in the city for ten years. I realize that even when I've been completely in love with city life, I've always held this idea that if I had more peace and quiet, and my own office, and a place to go for walks—some room for myself to spread out—that I would be a more productive writer and a healthier, more spiritual person. I have a feeling we're going to do it—it's almost as if we've started something we can't stop, as if our staying in the city somehow would be giving up.

It will be interesting to see what happens if we put ourselves to this test. I am a little worried about being isolated, about being with Nicky so much that we start to drive each other nuts. Most couples we know go to separate jobs and don't see each other until after work, whereas we'll be seeing each other all day long. So this house, I suppose, will either kill us or make us stronger. I'm going hot and cold on the whole thing—one minute wondering how I'm going to survive without Thai food deliveries and French movies, and the next thinking about how nice it would be to plant bulbs in the spring and to start a vegetable garden. And to have my own space to write and think.

∼

We've now had another look at the house and told the owners that we're going to take it. Yesterday we called both sets of parents to officially tell them that we're moving out of the city. My parents, of course, were thrilled to hear that we were finally getting out, choosing to live in a town that they might have chosen for themselves, and in a house that would have plenty of room for them to stay when they came to visit. Nicky's dad was a little less gung-ho, understandably; his son was leaving the big city and would no longer be a cab ride away. Even though we'll only be an hour's drive from Manhattan, there will always be a huge difference between living in the city and living outside of it. He is also concerned that we might lose some of our contacts and visibility in the writing world, or that we might feel isolated in a new place with no natural way to meet people. He has a point: since our workdays involve sitting at home in front of the computer, we're not going to see much of anyone but each other. Betsy was more enthusiastic. She loves gardening and walks and old houses, so she can't wait to see the place.

The other announcement we had for both families concerned our plans for the holidays. Over the past month or so I've been nagging Nicky about making an official, preemptive policy on Christmas visits. I wanted us to present a united front on the question of where we'd be this Christmas morning, so that we wouldn't find ourselves separately promising to be two places at once. We dismissed the idea of trying to travel back and forth between families, since they happen to live three-hundred miles apart. The idea of attempting to bring the families to our house was out of the question—not only were we planning to move in December, we weren't ready yet to play hosts. We finally decided the best thing to do would be to alternate our yearly celebration, and since I felt strongly about being with my mother and the rest of my family this first Christmas after our wedding, we agreed to spend this year's holiday at my parents' house in New Hampshire. Next year, we'll go to the Weinstocks here in New York.

Telling my folks was easy, since nothing would immediately change for them except for the happy addition of Nicky at the dinner table. Breaking the news to my new in-laws was harder. This would be the first time in nearly three decades that Nicky would not be around for the holidays. His brother, who lives in Moscow, would be home for just a couple of weeks. I didn't want Nicky's family to feel as if I were taking their son away from them. At the same time, because we're in the city, we spend a lot more time with Nicky's family than we do with mine, and I wanted to be sure my parents didn't feel that he was taking me away from them, either. In short, no matter how we looked at it, we felt like a pair of Grinches. Spending Christmas with the Beesleys automatically meant heartlessly blowing off Nicky's family, and vice versa next year. I know—we both know—that marriage necessitates changes, like valuing our personal needs and styles over those of our families, but we had no idea how to make those changes without hurting everyone's feelings.

Anyway, when we told them about our plans for Christmas, Nicky's parents were disappointed but didn't argue. At some point they probably had to make the same choice themselves. I'm not sure whether being married gives us more clout in the eyes of the world, or if it's just that we act more decisively now that we're married. It feels good, though. No need to pull a Bitchy Bride anymore; instead we simply say what we've decided, and it sticks.

~

A few weeks ago, I finally decided that I should stop being so passive—or maybe scared—and get some of my own information about dementia, so I signed up for an orientation meeting at the Alzheimer's Association. The meeting is today (in an hour, in fact) and I don't want to go. Nicky offered to come with me, which hadn't even occurred to me, since I generally think of this as *my* problem. I'm not sure why this is any different from me going to the hospital when Davis had his knee fixed, or when Betsy went in for her hip operation, but I know that the world responds differently to my mother's illness. It frightens people in a way that normal aging does not, maybe because it's so irrational. It makes sense that a woman who has jogged every day for fifty years might finally wear out a knee, or that a man who smoked a pack a day for his entire life would get emphysema. We can accept that the body eventually gives out, especially if there's some reason for it doing so. But to have no idea what day comes after Tuesday, or to not be able to read a watch, or to forget who's running the country, this threatens to subvert the delicate order we've imposed on this disorderly world. It threatens to take you next. I think this is why I don't talk about it much to others, and why I even half expect Nicky to look the other way. I know how scary it is to other people, and I don't really blame them for not knowing how to handle it.

(Later)

The orientation meeting was an ambush. When I signed up for it, I assumed it meant listening to a little presentation about the history of the Alzheimer's Association and picking up some literature on the services available. I wanted, and expected, to be anonymous; to quietly gather information and then leave without having made any promises to myself or anyone else. Instead, I found myself sitting around a table in a dimly lit room with about seven other people, all of them at least twenty years older than I. Planted in the center of the table, ominously, was a brand-new box of Kleenex. A woman not much older than me came into the room and introduced herself as our "facilitator." She asked us to go around the table, first giving our names and then saying why we were there. I've always hated this kind of thing. I started planning my response, which went something like this: *Hi, I'm Amanda, I'm a Libra, and my mother wears her undershirt outside of her sweater.* Why couldn't Miss Facilitator just turn off the lights and show us an informative video? I felt the usual combination of dread and stage fright as my turn to talk came up. What I thought was going to be a lecture was turning out to be a support group, with a nurturing, sympathetic moderator and a bunch of crying freaks. I say this only because I was one of them. I started blubbering as soon as I said my name, and for the next hour I couldn't stop. Thank God Nicky was there. It was overwhelming: I didn't know anyone, and I wasn't prepared to actually talk about my mother to all those strangers, since I wasn't really used to talking about her to anyone at all—including myself.

My new best friends told stories about wives who urinated on the kitchen floor, husbands who would only watch children's TV, and mothers who had forgotten their children's names. Because I was the youngest person in the group, and because my mother's behavior was not as dramatic as that of many of the loved ones being described, the entire discussion began to seem like a prophecy of what would happen as my mother's illness got worse. So the meeting represented both the promise of future suffering and the lamest of cures. I resented the grief of these strangers, their disappointments and loss, and I was angry at myself for opening myself up to their despair. The meeting was all wrong, somehow, not at all how I wanted to deal with my own sadness.

As the other people talked, I kept telling myself that at least my mother wasn't as bad as their mothers, their wives, their husbands. As if this were a competition that I, or my mom, could somehow win.

To make matters worse, I had planned my day so that as soon as I left the building, I had to go to lunch with my new editor at *Self*. I said good-bye to Nicky and began to walk, sniveling and splotchy from crying. I felt drained and vulnerable. I arrived at the restaurant early and went into the bathroom to clean up and put on some makeup. As I splashed my face with water, I promised myself that from now on I'd give myself more space to deal with all this sadness. I'm not going to pretend that this isn't serious anymore, that I'm in control of everything I feel.

By the time we sat down for lunch I had pulled myself together. My editor was very nice and not scary at all. I'm so glad to have this job, to be on track as a writer, to be having lunch and pretending, like everyone else in the restaurant, that I have my shit together.

~

I'm sure I have dementia. I start sentences and don't finish them. I forget to call people back. The youngest known case of Alzheimer's occurred in someone who was twenty-eight, so it's not impossible. This, of course, is all after-shock from the meeting yesterday.

The more likely explanation for my spaciness is that I'm totally stressed out. Isn't moving up there on the list of stressful activities, somewhere between driving a New York cab and getting divorced? All I know is I can't stop thinking about what size truck we need, how we should pack, whether the house will need any fixing up, etc. etc. This all late at night, of course. If it's not a wedding, I'll come up with something to stay awake thinking about.

~

I can't wait to move to the country. For Nicky. For the dog. For me.

In the mail today, between the seven copies of the same Victoria's Secret catalog that I've *never* ordered from, was a letter calling me to jury duty for the day we're supposed to move. As I read over the thing, I freaked out. I stormed around the apartment, kicking boxes and cursing about this moronic city and its inane system of twisted laws. Then I called the county clerk's office in a frenzy, bypassing the automated answering system by pressing the zero button over and over. As soon as the receptionist picked up, I screamed, "Don't you *dare* put me on hold!" I told her I couldn't go to jury duty. I yelled that I was about to move, that I wouldn't even be *living* in New York City by December 1. The woman on the phone was calm and professional. Between my frantic protestations about packing books and calling the cable guy, she managed to explain that the entire business of getting out of serving is really a very simple one, that all I had to do was fax or mail them a copy of my new lease. She gave me the number and told me not to worry.

I felt like a creep. I told the lady all about our new house, the horses in the field, and how I couldn't wait to get out of the city. "I want to plant bulbs," I told her. I apologized for flipping out. I'm sure she had me on speakerphone in the office and that everyone was laughing at me, the wack job who shrieks about tulips. I can't explain why it happened. It was as if everything that was difficult in my life—the column deadlines, the move, all the stuff about my mom—was all concentrated in that flimsy piece of paper asking me to serve on a jury for three days starting on December 1.

~

Dinner with Tara and David tonight, which left me feeling grumpy and mean. As usual, they were insufferably condescending toward us, with their predictions that we should expect a very difficult first year of marriage. When we told them about the house we'd found, and about moving, they had a lukewarm reaction. David told us how they, too, had thought about leaving the city once they got married, but had decided against it because they realized they'd be too bored. As we were leaving, Tara took me aside and told me how she didn't know if our move was such a good idea. "The first year of marriage is really *hard*," she said. "We

146

had a lot of problems. We needed support. You might want to wait a little while before you move."

Even though I knew it was a stupid thing to say, I couldn't shake it off. When we got home, everything we had seemed shabby. Nicky put on the TV, and as we watched yet another sitcom repeat, I felt angry at him because we were watching TV, angry at the TV for being so loud, angry at myself for letting Tara get to me.

Our apartment is out of control, with boxes piled in every corner and the dust building up. Why clean when you're going to move in a month? As I write, the people in the apartment downstairs are having a noisy party. I should be happy because I know we're moving, but I'm just irritated.

The only thing that has made me feel good lately was our going to help Karen move into her new apartment in Yonkers yesterday. I was proud of Nicky, proud that I could share him with a friend, proud that he could carry the chest of drawers all by himself, proud that he was willing to help without getting all macho-moving-man about the whole thing. Once we got everything upstairs, we all sat around her living room floor and ate sandwiches, and Karen seemed really excited about her new place. The best thing about moving is the idea, however unrealistic, of a clean slate. You can daydream about inventing a whole new life for yourself, one in which you go for hikes and throw dinner parties, bake bread and write beautiful things all day long.

I think Tara's going to be wrong about this. So far, two months after our wedding day, marriage is the easy part. It's the rest of life that's hard.

~

Suddenly I feel like Lois Lane in the newsroom, with edits due this week on my first column and a new one due by the end of the week. It feels great to have deadlines, especially ones that have nothing to do with card games.

I keep thinking that things are going to calm down now that we're done with the wedding and the honeymoon and almost caught up with thank-you notes for the wedding presents still trickling in. But now there's the move, and next there will be something else. I guess I thought that getting married, after a single life of running around alone in a storm, would feel like coming into a cozy room with a huge fireplace. It's not. Getting married means still being in the middle of the storm—but, instead of being alone, having someone to put his arm around you when it gets really nasty. It's not all about being happy, I realize, as if putting rings on our fingers would somehow make everything in the world perfect, but more about progress, crossing one big thing off a lifetime list of things to do.

Julia called and asked if I wanted to meet her for a quick dinner today, and I realized as we were talking that she expected Nicky would come along as well. Before we were married, this would have seemed normal to me: Julia and Nicky are friends. But lately I'm feeling very territorial about *my* friends, *my* space, and *my* stuff. I'm not used to people assuming that Nicky and I will always come as a unit, even though most of the time we do. It's time to get used to having that arm around me. And to politely throwing it off when it feels suffocating.

~

I've been thinking about what Tara said the other night, trying to figure out exactly why I reacted so strongly to her hushed warning about the first year of marriage. Maybe it's because she hit on something: I'm half afraid we're going to be saddled with new marital problems along with our new front porch. Half the time I can't remember why we decided to do it in the first place. The house is starting to seem less adorable in my memory. Was it my imagination or was the roof about to collapse? Naturally, for the past couple days the city has been idyllic, full of wise bums, friendly pit bulls, and adorable children eating messy candy on their way to school.

After Tara's dire warning about marital strife, I've been asking everyone I know about our plan to move, weighing their responses against hers. Nobody else has echoed her concern, although a number of people have nodded sagely and said, "You're in a nesting phase." This is a new one to me. I like to think our decision to move isn't just some kind of knee-jerk, animal-kingdom reaction to getting married, but they're probably right. I'm just not crazy about the word "nesting." Sounds like dirty feathers.

~

We've had our first big fight, although I'm not sure Nicky noticed. This past weekend we went to Providence to have dinner with a bunch of Nicky's friends from college and their wives. It was something he'd planned a long time ago, and now that the date had arrived, I was dreading it. I had a column to write, and the move was just two weeks away. It wasn't that I didn't like his friends, who were all sweet guys; it just seemed crazy to be leaving for the weekend when we had so much to do. On the morning we were supposed to leave, I was in a foul mood about making the trip and trying not to take it out on Nicky, since it wasn't really his fault. They were his friends, true, but I had agreed to go with him over a month ago. And besides, we were married now. Isn't this the kind of thing a wife is supposed to do with her husband?

We dragged our bags and coats and a book on tape and some snacks out to the outdoor parking lot where we kept my car. I got behind the wheel and prepared to back out as Nicky waited on the sidewalk, ready to give me the signal when the street was clear. When he waved for me to move, I backed straight out and smacked the passenger side door into a fire hydrant. Nicky came over to look. It's nothing, he said. No big deal. So I got out and took a look for myself. What he thought was nothing was a huge *dent* in the side of my car! Incredulous, I asked Nicky what had happened, how he could wave me back without seeing that I was going to hit something. He explained that he was looking for traffic on the street and not paying attention to what was happening on the sidewalk. As if it were my fault for not being more careful.

It was not a good start to the trip. As we set off toward the highway, I didn't say anything. Neither did he. I was waiting for an apology; that was all I wanted. But he wasn't talking. Finally I asked, "Are you going to say you're sorry?"

He seemed surprised. "I assumed you knew I was sorry," he said. "Of course I didn't do it on purpose."

I told him I knew he didn't do it on purpose, but I needed him to say he was sorry anyway.

"I'm sorry the car got dented," he said.

In the face of such profound soul-searching, what could I say? For the next hour neither of us spoke. I could tell that he was waiting for me to say something, and that if I didn't, he would remain quietly reproachful of my anger for the rest of the trip. This is one of the little ugly patterns of our relationship: whenever I get mad, Nicky gets quiet; and this only makes me angrier, because it sticks me with the responsibility of bringing everything into the open, of opening the lines of communication and "talking things out." Well, this time, I didn't feel like making it easy. I had been put out in the first place by having to go on this trip, and then further insulted by being directed to drive into a hydrant and ruin my car. (OK, it wasn't ruined.) I was the one being wronged here. I wanted some credit. As usual, it fell to me to make the first move. I told him that it would have made me feel better about the trip if he had acknowledged that it was a bad time for us to be going and thanked me for coming with him. I said I knew the dent wasn't his fault, but it was still his responsibility. The funny thing is, as I explained how I felt, I realized that none of it was news to him. It just didn't occur to him to *say* anything to me. Men are very strange. They'd rather drive in silence for an hour than say I'm sorry.

The dinner itself turned out to be exactly as I expected: the men talked about the old days—parties in the dorm rooms, crazy roommates, stealing food from the cafeteria—and the women laughed at their stories about eating six pizzas and falling out of cars. Ah, the glory of someone else's college experiences. In situations like this, I'm usually drawn to the quietest person in the room, the one who's too shy to say anything boring. In this case, I spent most of the evening talking to one of the wives about her teaching job. At least I learned something.

Strangely, as we said our good-byes, knowing it would

be another year before we saw each other again, it felt good to have done this favor for Nicky, to have been perfectly wifelike. The only problem was not being the kind of wife I like.

~

Last night I dreamed that I parked the car in the driveway of our new house, and when I got out of the car a wolf came charging at me from the woods. It jumped on me like a friendly dog, but I knew that it wanted to hurt me.

My first thought was that this was just an anxiety dream about moving, but then I wondered if maybe the wolf-dog represents the part of me that wants to be wild and free. The part of me that wants to be different, that doesn't want to go to happy little dinners and make nice with everyone in the room. I'm afraid of that side of me, so I make it scary, give it the form of a dangerous animal. Part of me is afraid that bad things happen to people who are different. Mom was different, and look what happened to her. Maybe if I just act like everyone else, I'll grow old like everyone else. Then again, wouldn't it be better to be different now and simply forget it later than to be a conformist now and remember that failure for the rest of my life?

I just remembered that Mom once told me she doesn't dream. I wonder if she ever did, and if so, what stories those dreams told.

~

We've been packing all day. As usual, I'm acting very picky about my stuff. At one point Nicky picked up my framed picture of Wonder Woman and asked, "Do you want this packed with the other pictures?" And instead of acting like a normal person I snapped, "Don't touch that." As if it were a family heirloom or something. Lately I get really touchy about the way Nicky folds my laundry, and I hate it when he leaves things on my desk, like old magazines or letters, even bills that I'm supposed to pay. I seem to be reacting to the idea that I am now expected to share everything with him, from my books to my body, and even though I know this isn't true, that this isn't what he's expecting, I can't help fighting it anyway. I'm not sure how to define my space now that we're married. It's not like anything has physically changed—we still have our own clothes, our own desks, our personal favorite books, all the stuff that we care about separately—but emotionally I want to stake my claims early, to make it clear what I consider private and my own before it gets subsumed by our communal marriage.

~

The house is now full of boxes and we're down to the very worst part of packing—deciding what to do with the stupid bits and pieces. I've got one hundred mix tapes that I never listen to, favorite sweaters I no longer wear, a one-cup coffeemaker from when I lived alone, and several boxes of letters and cards received over the years. I guess I should throw all of it in the trash, part of the streamlining of my new life. At the same time, I don't want to leave my old life in the dust. It's the downside of having a perfectly matched set of plates: you've got to get rid of the mismatched ones. I ended up throwing almost everything out, but I did keep the letters. I figure by the time we're grandparents, with the role of advancing technology, no one will even know what a letter is anymore, and they will be conversation pieces.

Emma is freaked out by all the packing, and I have to admit that I am too.

(Garrison)

Well, we're here. We've been up since 6:30 A.M., and we're exhausted; but our bamboo welcome mat from Chinatown (adorned with the Chinese character for "double-luck") is outside the front screen door, which must mean we've moved.

Nicky's brother Luke is in the guest room, watching TV. He helped us with the move, carrying boxes and alphabetizing novels in the bookshelf. It was great having him. Otherwise I think Nicky and I would be a little disconcerted our first night here in the middle of nowhere.

155

What if the wolf-dog decided to come out of my dreams for a real visit?

Now to set about the task of turning this house into a home, our first home as a married couple. I feel like we're pioneers together, staking our claim on a new part of the world. It's cold outside, and instead of being in an over-heated apartment, we're in an old, drafty house with pipes that threaten to freeze. Everything is in our hands now. We are no longer newly wedded, but newly married, and somehow the distinction is clear. Where our life together used to be about our dreams, now it's about the work necessary to make them a reality. We're trying to shove along our careers, to set up a new home, to build a bonfire out of the small pile of twigs we've gathered together along the way.

PART THREE

The Marriage

Over the past twelve months, I had been a legal secretary, fiancée, ghostwriter, wedding planner, bride, playwright, honeymooner, magazine columnist, and new wife. On top of that, I turned thirty, which thankfully meant that I no longer had to worry about all the things I wouldn't accomplish before then. My twenties were finally behind me, a mixed-up decade of wrangling with who I was, of blind dates and beer, of career changes and shifts in friendships. You couldn't pay me to go back to those days; but for the very same reasons that it was a relief, turning thirty was also a drag. I had chosen a career and promised myself not to give up. I had chosen a companion and promised him I'd never leave. I was in no danger of being discovered by a famous film director while sitting in a coffee shop. I was never going to become a foreign correspondent for CNN. I had made certain choices that are going to determine the course of my life. And as reasonable and well thought out as I knew these choices were, I was aware that making them meant leaving certain things behind. Most things, actually.

Nicky and I had become a family, in charge of our own decisions and responsible for each other. My parents and brothers, who had always been the nucleus of my family, were now in orbit of this other, more important relationship. It was strange to see evidence of this shift in power, to think of ourselves as the new generation. From the moment of our wedding, looking out for our parents was no longer something we did for extra credit: it was part of the job description. I felt more protective than ever of my parents and of my in-laws, and I knew that they would eventually lean on us just as we had leaned on them.

There were changes in our social life, too. Nicky and I seemed to be spending the majority of our time with other married or almost-married couples. This, I suppose, was to be expected: there's something all-American and gloriously easy about a couple of couples, with their solid four-walls construction and built-in variety of options. The women can make the drinks while the guys marinade the chops, and there can be endless cross-couple conversations and flirtations. I'd always loved double dates, ever since high school when Barbara and I dated Conrad and Elliot: we drank beer in garages and commandeered tables at Mc-Donald's, creating what are still some of my fondest memories of my hometown social life. Still, I wanted to keep friendships that were mine alone, independent from Nicky, and would have been more than happy if he did the same. But maintaining those friendships suddenly seemed more complicated.

I hadn't completely forgone my single friends in favor of a couples-only club, but as soon as we got married, or maybe sometime the year before, Nicky and I became a social unit. People didn't just invite one of us out anymore; it was always both. I began to feel sentimental for the days when a girls' night didn't have a name—when just about every night presented a choice between boy and friend. Then again, in those days I thought it was fun to go to noisy bars and drink cheap beer. Things had changed and were still changing, which was not altogether a bad thing. The hard part was trying to keep up.

All of my relationships seemed to have shifted and settled in the wake of marriage. Not only were we spending more time with other couples, but the couples were not at all who I would have expected them to be. I was sure, for instance, that Tara and her new husband would be our lifelong friends, the twosome that would make us the sort of foursome featured on table-wine commercials and board-game boxes. After all, Tara and I had great singles chemistry. Over the years we'd celebrated new jobs and commiserated over breakups, cooked each other dinner, and spent time with each other's families. I had us pegged for tandem childbirth in our thirties and swapping photos of grandchildren in our sixties. But what I learned is that singles chemistry does not necessarily carry over to married life. Since our weddings, Tara and I remained polite friends, but our couples chemistry never got off the ground. As a result, we saw each other much less than we used to. The opposite thing happened when Natalie, an old girlfriend of Nicky's, got married. I wouldn't have expected to become tight with her or her boyfriend, Paul. But after both our weddings, the four of us seemed to have become united in holy friendship, and they were suddenly counted as the closest of friends.

Part of the intensity of couples chemistry was the feeling of our having all joined a secret society: the major leagues, as it were, of coupledom. When my husband and I were at dinner with another married couple, each of the four of us knew not only what we would have as a main course, but whom we'd be eating main courses across from for the next fifty years. We were bound by this knowledge, and awed by it. It was completely different from being out with a close friend, though; when Nicky and I went out with a couple, I didn't expect to hear anything from the wife that the husband didn't already know. If I was alone with a married friend, however, the rules were different: then we'd *really* talk, although rarely with the same lack of restraint as in a conversation between single friends.

Being married was also making me more comfortable with letting go of friendships that had stopped being fun. I had begun to think in terms of consolidating and streamlining my life. At last I owned a decent set of plates that made me feel neat, pleased, and well taken care of; so it shouldn't have been surprising that I found myself wanting a decent set of friends, single and married, who did the same. It's funny how my tastes changed: guys who might have seemed boring to me in the singles scene appeared wise and good-husbandly when I was with them and their wives. Women who once would have struck me as brassy and domineering seemed the heroic heads of households now that they were married. And my oldest friends from high school and college became more and more important to me, because they knew me single and married and had stuck by me the whole time.

But even with all this new self-awareness, I still felt the ground beneath us was as shaky as ever. I was glad we had each other to hang on to.

DECEMBER

Barely slept last night. The wind was whining through the edges of the window and I woke up freezing at 2:00 A.M. Nighttime is scary in the country. It gets so dark that I can't even see Emma when I take her out for her after-dinner walk. All night my brain was whirling with all the things I still have to do, all the things we're going to have to buy, all the money we will now have to spend on heating and snowplowing and fixing up the living room. It was one of those nights that went on forever.

I realize I've never lived in the country before. I'm not used to total darkness, and branches that fall for no reason, and the scurrying noises of small animals in the bushes. Hard-core country folk would laugh at me for even calling this town the country, seeing as it's only an hour's drive from New York City. But from what I can tell, this place counts as the real thing, with its hay fields and horses and our woodburning stove. Suddenly, New York seems so safe, always lit up and always open. Around here, you couldn't see an ax murderer if he were limping down the road toward your house.

(Later)

Feeling much better with the light of day. I'm sitting at my desk in my study in my (that is, *our*) new house. I read somewhere that after a mother gives birth one of the first things she'll do is examine her baby from head to foot. That's how I feel about this house: I just had a few minutes alone while Nicky was at the store, and I ran my hands along the old tin walls of my study, listened to the snap of a log burning in the woodstove, and shuffle-danced around the house in my sweat socks and overalls.

I'm so proud of us. We were both curious about life in a new place, so we packed up and moved here. It feels like a victory. A bonus of being married is the thrill of self-sufficiency. We're a mobile unit, a team now. We can go anywhere we want, as long as we're together.

∼

As though it had decided to wait until the moment when we actually depended on it for more than an occasional weekend away, the car died on the way to the grocery store. The mechanic says the repairs are going to be expensive. Why couldn't this have happened as we were leaving for Providence last month?

It has been snowing on and off for the past couple of days, which has made our house more beautiful and more lonely than ever. I took a walk with Emma, and it was quiet and clean because of the snow. I forgot all about the car and the deadline of my upcoming column. At least I did for fifteen minutes. I lay down in the snow, made a snow angel, and was very glad there was no one around to see me.

We've borrowed Nicky's brother's Jeep while the mechanic works on ours. I drove into town bundled in blankets (it's more of a summertime car), and at the grocery store I saw Allan, the guy who used to live in our house, the one who was going to be our best friend and have us over for dinner. When I saw him he said again how much he wanted us to get together, but I could tell he didn't mean it. As I smiled politely and said, "That sounds *great*," I marveled at my old misconception that people in the country have a lower bullshit factor than they do in the city. Boy, was I wrong.

~

It's so quiet.

We've been here for two weeks now, and life is starting to feel a little more normal. Only a few more boxes remain unpacked. In between bursts of writing I've been plastering and painting the ceiling in the guest bedroom, which we agreed to do in exchange for a slightly lower rent. I've also been taking biweekly trips to Wal-Mart to stock up on necessary supplies for the house: light bulbs, mousetraps (unfortunately), long matches for the woodstove, a curtain for the bathroom window, a handheld shower attachment for the bathtub. And on the way home I stop at thrift shops for all the unnecessary things, like a little throw rug, a lamp, a bedside table, and a few used books about Joan of Arc, my latest female role model.

Nicky has been going into the city two or three times a week, where he's a member of a library that gives him a desk for writing, so we are not around each other as much as I expected. I haven't been as motivated to go in—it feels strange being an outsider, walking the streets without a home base a few blocks away. Last week I went in to have lunch with a friend, and it was so cold that I ended up buying long underwear and putting it on in the bathroom of a Barnes & Noble. Already I've lost my city legs, forgetting to go prepared with a hat and the right clothes.

So now with Nicky gone a few days a week and me at home, messing around with curtains and spackle in between magazine columns, I'm a little bored. My old writing projects feel stale, and I haven't been inspired to start any new ones. I'm thinking of joining a not-so-nearby gym to get in shape, and signing up for a pottery class so maybe I'll meet some people. Yuck. It feels so artificial to have to set out to meet people, but how else do you do it when you're an adult? It's not like there's a dorm party every weekend. This is one drawback to the joyful self-sufficiency of being married.

Nicky's parents came out to see us two weekends ago,

bearing smoked salmon, good coffee, and bagels. We took a walk around the property—it was a perfectly beautiful winter day—then came home for a New York City–style brunch. Davis has become much more excited about the place since he and Luke, Nicky's brother, heard that there is an excellent golf course in town. I think we'll be seeing more of them this spring. Betsy gave me quick lessons in choosing slipcovers and forcing amaryllis bulbs.

My folks came last weekend with their sleeping bags and a big can of maple syrup. That about sums up the difference between our families. Mom was in good spirits, and my father loves the place, of course. Nicky is so adorably son-in-lawish around my parents. As he fired up the woodstove this morning, he and Dad had a long conversation about chimney fires, cord prices, and snowplowing. Later, he took Mom to feed carrots to the horses while I put on the tea.

~

Last night when Nicky got home from the city, I was really awful to him—snappy and irritated. I'm beginning to realize how lonely it is to work by yourself, a fact which I had always heard was true but never quite understood until just lately. When I worked in publishing, I used to be jealous of all the writers who didn't have to get dressed up for work and deal with office politics every day. Now I'm jealous of those who do. I'm also envious of Nicky, who has managed to come out here without really moving all of himself. He still spends two or three days writing in the city, and then he'll have an after-work drink with a friend, and he plays basketball on 112th Street every Wednesday night—all while I sit here with Emma in the stillness of the house. I know I could go into the city, but I feel that the more I go in, the more it looks like defeat, and I won't give the urban naysayers the satisfaction.

As a result, Nicky is adjusting more easily to this move than I am—he's so positive about everything, whereas from time to time I'll allow myself to wallow in the miserable idea that we've made a huge mistake by moving. I don't tell Nicky what I'm thinking, since he would never let himself think that way. He plays the part of the stalwart optimist, and I bring up the disaster scenarios. The husband blindly plows ahead and the wife overthinks. What a couple.

We're still working out kinks, juggling the use of the borrowed Jeep and dividing chores that we never used to have (like laundry, which we used to drop off, and all the cooking, which we hardly did in the city). We're also trying to balance ourselves, to create an even-keeled *us*. It bothers me, I have to admit, that Nicky has yet to stay home while I'm off doing something in the city. I want him to spend a day in the house and know what it's like. Small-minded of me, I know, but it's true. If isolation is a part of marriage, then I want both of us to experience it. I don't want to be alone in my aloneness. I wonder if feeling isolated is typically female—we are, after all, better at forming relationships in the first place, so I'd imagine women would notice first if those relationships were missing. Or else, it's just me. The loner. Worse than that: the lonely wife.

~

The dog took a dump in my office yesterday. Seeing a pile of dung in the middle of my work space seemed somehow symbolic. It got me into a funk, and for the rest of the day everything was black. I didn't want Nicky to try to cheer me up, so I was deliberately evasive about what was bothering me. I've been so dark and dreary lately. Is this what Tara was talking about when she said that the first year of marriage was going to be hard? Damn her.

Anyway, Christmas is upon us. The goose is getting fat. So am I. We leave tomorrow for New Hampshire.

JANUARY

Back from what was probably the best Christmas we've ever had as a family, once everyone made it in through the snowstorms and delayed flights. We went on long hikes by day and cooked big dinners in the quiet, snowbound evenings. One night Jessie, Gordon's girlfriend, played a violin duet with my dad, and another night we went out and did Scottish reels at a neighbor's house. There was something very relaxed about it all, different from other family Christmases, and I think it had everything to do with my mother. She was dazzlingly happy to have the house full of people and music, and we were all so relieved to see that she was happy that it made us feel the same way. It had been a year since I read the letter with her diagnosis, and although she clearly wasn't getting better—in fact, she'd become markedly more dependent on my father since last year—at least she was still smiling and active and very much alive. The letter wasn't a death sentence after all, I realized. It was great to be around all these people, my people: husband, brothers and their loves, mother and father. It was almost perfect.

After Christmas dinner, we took turns playing selections from my mother's sizable collection of seventies rock and pop albums. At one point we were all dancing to "Car Wash" next to the Christmas tree. It wasn't like old times; it was better. Dad was spinning Mom around, Nicky and I were doing the Bump, and everyone was laughing.

~

(Back Home)

Now that our routines are settling in, Nicky and I both work at home more frequently. Unlike the setup in our old apartment, where our desks were separated by a thin wall and I could hear Nicky tapping on his keyboard, now we have entire rooms between our offices. To avoid having to yell across the house, we bought intercoms from Radio Shack. Now when I'm hungry, I can buzz Nicky and see if he'd like to meet me in the kitchen for lunch. And when it's time to get the mail, Nicky can invite me to take a walk with him to the mailbox (the highlight of my day). My favorite intercom buzz is the one at five that signals that it's time for a glass of wine. We put on music and cook dinner together, and the city feels a million miles away.

But for the past few days, Nicky has seemed tense and a little unhappy. Just as I become more of an optimist, he takes over as the local pessimist. Maybe the move has been harder on him than I thought, or maybe I haven't given enough consideration to how it's affecting him. Maybe his novel isn't ending as quickly or as well as he'd like. He's the strong one all the time, the one who always looks on the bright side, and I'm always having some sort of crisis. Now that the tables are turning, I'm surprised to see him fall into my role. Maybe I need to give him more airtime to complain, to hand it to him or even force it on him— he never seems to take it for himself.

~

At one point this afternoon I realized I had gone the entire day without talking to anyone except Emma. Nicky was in the city, and I had worked all day at resurrecting this one-act play I've been writing for a hundred years. I was wearing old sweats and sneakers, and I had put my hair back without brushing it first, and when I caught a glimpse of myself in the mirror I was actually scared. I decided to go into town and take a walk, maybe have a cup of coffee. I brushed my hair and put on jeans and a pair of shoes. I drove into town and walked into the local luncheonette to get a cappuccino. There was no one there. Their cappuccino machine was broken, so I ordered a cup of tea and sat there by myself, trying to figure out whether being alone in a luncheonette is any better than being alone at home. When I got home I signed onto the Internet, and, for the first time in my life, went to a chat room. There was no one else there. I was virtually alone as well.

I hope we haven't made a mistake by moving out here. I don't want to have to admit that I can't figure out what's good for me and what's not.

~

I continue to throw all my energy into tasks around the house. I order curtains for the kitchen, reglue the peeling wallpaper in the bathroom, buy new blinds for the dining room, and trim the fur around Emma's eyes. I remember that it's time to change the sheets, and on the way to the basement where the washing machine is, I notice that our silver teapot needs polishing. I polish the teapot and move on to the silver candlesticks. Then I feel a little hungry. I wish I had a cinnamon roll. I pull out a cookbook and start flipping through it. Halfway through dissolving a package of yeast in lukewarm water for the cinnamon rolls, I realize that I have forgotten about the laundry. In total frustration, I scrap the cinnamon roll project and the clothes-washing idea and take a walk instead.

Even Nicky has the homemaking bug. Yesterday morning I was reading the paper in Nicky's office. Nicky got up from his desk, left, and came back a few minutes later with a dark, heavy piece of fabric from the basement. He began to tack this cloth over the window facing his desk. I asked him what he was doing.

"I don't like people being able to see in," he said. "It's too open."

"But that's cutting off all your light," I said.

"It's all right."

"It's awful," I said. "You need a curtain to cover the bottom half of the window. That way the light will come in, but you'll still have your privacy."

And without giving him a chance to fully digest this rather advanced interior design concept, I sprang out of my chair and began rummaging through my magazine pile for a picture to show him. Seeing that I had taken over, Nicky went back to work.

As I pored over the *Country Curtains* catalog, it hit me that I was taking on another job, distracting myself yet again from my work and threatening my sanity. I exhaled loudly. Nicky didn't look away from his computer screen.

I huffed and rattled the pages of the magazine. Finally I threw the thing across the room. In answer to Nicky's wary inquiry, I began listing everything I'd done over the past week, including this. I explained that we weren't finished making the house look nice, that unpacking was only the *first* step in making it ours, and if he wasn't going to help in some way, I was going to go nuts. I could tell he saw my point, but he clearly didn't want to talk about it right then. His whole body was turned toward his computer, and his hands were still resting on the keyboard. I suggested that we think about it and talk sometime soon. He agreed immediately.

I went to my office and worked for a few hours, and at lunchtime came into the kitchen and found him on the phone. "I want a tier for a thirty-three-inch window," he was saying. "Sheer ivory, no edging on that. And a brass spring rod."

I was impressed. This is the man who normally wouldn't think of changing the sheets until it looks as though Emma is asleep on the bed—even when she isn't. As I listened to him debate the virtues of muslin versus cotton voile with a sales representative, I understood that my husband is perfectly capable of accomplishing domestic task work without my help—and is in fact more likely to do so when I don't interfere. Or at least when I only interfere a little.

Today I returned from *my* day in the city to find that while I was off catching a movie with a friend, Nicky had baked brownies, swept the kitchen, washed the dog, folded a load of laundry, started cooking dinner, and planned dessert. I appreciated the gesture, which seemed to be a kind of apology. This is typically Nicky: rather than talking about problems or apologizing for screwups, he prefers to go out and *fix* them. Sometimes it works, and sometimes it doesn't, but this was a clear victory. Brownies and laundry go a lot further than "talking it out" for an hour, that's for sure.

FEBRUARY

I finally joined a gym, which offered a free "fitness test" along with the membership. I made the mistake of agreeing to do the test right away, and a seventeen-year-old beefcake flashed his dimples and took me into a little room. Then he hooked me up to a contraption which spit out a report saying that I'm fifteen pounds heavier than I thought, made up almost exclusively of fat, and an inch shorter than when last measured. And then there was this stupid lung-tester machine that I was supposed to blow into, which broke as soon as I tried it. It was awful. How do you exercise after news like that? I sat in the whirlpool instead, where the short, heavy people go.

It's the Freshman Fifteen revisited, only I haven't been eating pints of ice cream every night or chugging beer at keg parties. I don't want to be a dumpy wife. Nicky hasn't gained any weight at all; in fact, he looks better than when I first met him. Sit-ups every morning, basketball once a week. I know I'm never going to have that kind of discipline, but I'm going to have to figure something out.

When I came home in a total funk, Nicky insisted, as he always does, that I am beautiful and sexy and just perfect in every way. This, of course, isn't true, and I informed him of that. He protested, I accused him of making nice to make me feel better, and after a few more minutes of this inane back-and-forth, he threw up his hands, stormed out of the bedroom, and flipped on the television to watch skinny girls have catfights on *Melrose Place*. I'm on a conveyor belt to hell: first I become this happy and chubby newly married Amanda, and before I know it I'll be pregnant, and after that all I've got to look forward to is hips permanently spread, breasts down to my ankles, and a serious turkey neck.

∼

Things I do to avoid working:

1. clean up my desk
2. order stuff from catalogs and then return them
3. think of things I want next Christmas
4. cook huge and complicated lunches
5. write e-mails
6. make lists

MARCH

Am finally feeling less isolated out here. It helps going to the gym, taking classes, all the things you know you're supposed to do when you move to a new town but it's not so easy to actually do them. I'm feeling good about my writing too. The columns are going well, and I've been working away on the poor little one-act in my spare time.

My memory gets worse whenever I try to talk about Mom. I was trying to tell someone the name of the drug she was taking, and I couldn't remember it for the life of me. It's like my brain freezes up on the subject. Maybe in empathy. Maybe in imitation. Maybe in denial.

~

I watched a nature show on TV last night, and then I dreamed about bears. I was walking along a snowy white beach, and I knew there were white bears hidden in the snow. The special had explained that bears don't usually attack unless you invade their personal space, so I was scared to continue walking because I couldn't see where the bears were hiding. I woke up thinking about Mom. Just recently I wrote her sister in England to keep her up to date on Mom's condition (something that's difficult for Dad to do since he is with her all the time and she doesn't want to talk about it—or overhear anyone else do so). Auntie Sylvia is always grateful for news about how her little sister is doing, and I know it's helpful, but still I feel guilty about doing it, as if I were betraying Mom somehow: the daughter-turned-informant. I even feel bad when I talk about Mom to close friends. It's as if every time I vocally acknowledge the situation I'm making it more real. Or maybe I see it as giving up hope that something might change for the better—even though I know in my heart that such a change is unlikely.

I think this dream means that I'm afraid that by talking about Mom behind her back, by invading her personal space, she'll fight back by being angry. I also think that I—and everyone who loves Mom—is in a no-win situation.

~

My new husband is always saving people. Wherever he goes, he ends up helping old ladies cross the street, carrying strollers up the subway steps, or driving kids to the hospital when they've fallen off their bikes. I think it's his calling, so it was not a surprise to me when Nicky joined the volunteer fire department in town. Once or twice a week, he gets a call on his pager at 3:00 A.M. and speeds off into the night, returning at dawn with stories of cutting open a car door with the Jaws of Life, or putting out a brush fire, or investigating a smoky attic. How sexy is that?

I love being a fireman's wife and having my lover come home smelling of sweat and smoke, especially as it's only a part-time job.

In turn, I joined a little society of my own, at least for the day—the well-trained emergency response team at the local beauty parlor. While Nicky traded made-up fishing stories and car-fire memories with the guys at the station, I schooled myself in local gossip over highlights and a trim. I even met a fellow wife-of-a-firefighter there, and we laughed about what a cliché we had accidentally become. Suddenly I saw my future: spending weekends with the beauty salon ladies; making cookies for the fire department bake sale while the men hosed down the pumper; cooking up huge pots of chili for the guys as they settled around the TV for a big game. I found myself wondering what happened to the tomboy in me, the only girl on the soccer and baseball teams when I was a kid, an ardent feminist in college. Why wasn't I the only girl in the volunteer fire department? Just because I wore a white dress and participated in a relatively traditional wedding, did that doom me to become a traditional wife?

In some ways, I think the answer is yes. And not only because I do the laundry and Nicky brings in the firewood. I do the laundry because I happen to have mastered an inexplicable method which involves removing certain articles before drying and others when barely dry, as well as washing special sweaters alone and several shirts with special detergent. Nicky brings in the firewood every morning during the winter, not only because he gets up earlier than I do and likes to get the woodstove going, but also because I don't stack it neatly enough when I bring it in. Yet our chores around the house aren't split along strict gender lines. I am in charge of everything to do with our car, from washing it to checking the oil. Nicky does almost all of the cooking, and he usually cleans the bathroom (largely, I think, because as a guy he looks into the toilet more often than I do and notices when it needs a scrub). I take care of the dishes and vacuuming; he does our recycling and touch-up painting. Last week he cleaned out the basement; the other day I put a new screen on our front door. We both have careers which we love, and we consider them to be equally important. In this way, I think we're a typical modern, newly married couple, ditching old-fashioned roles in favor of what we're actually good at.

Still, there are trends that make me feel, disappointingly, like a typical wife—silent assignments that are more subtle than the cooking and the cleaning. For instance, I find myself responsible for our relationship's emotional well-being. If Nicky and I argue, it's up to me to figure out what went wrong and how to talk about it. As the wife, I also seem to be in charge of most of the planning and daydreaming about our future: when we might have a kid, where and when we might buy a house, whether we could ever swing living in Italy for a year. Communication with our families has also become my job, keeping them up to date on what we're doing and figuring out when we'll see them next.

As for Nicky, he has his own quiet traditions to up-hold. He may not stand on the front porch and watch for intruders with a shotgun in his hands, but he does feel an incredible burden to protect the two of us. Although I'm the incurable analyzer of my dreams, he's the one who has nightmares about our new family in jeopardy. If I feel slighted by a friend, that friend instantly finds herself on Nicky's bad side. Although we share our money and seem to take turns with our career slouches and successes, it's clear that Nicky puts more pressure on himself to provide for the two of us than he puts on me. This seems to be true of most men, and I think most women encourage it. Nearly every married woman I know has said to me about her husband, "He will always make more money than me; it's just the way our careers have worked out." This simply isn't true with Nicky and me; there's no telling who might end up with more success as a writer. Anything could happen. So I try to remind him that we're in this together, that either one of us might end up carrying the other, or that we both may end up in totally different careers, but in any case, we're equally responsible for our family's success. It's not easy; we're both fighting to overcome what we've learned is the way the modern world works: a woman ought to have a career, but a man must earn most of the money.

~

Last night I dreamed that my Dad told me he had plans to go away and would be leaving Mom at home. I knew that I had to go and be with her, but I didn't want to. The dream left me feeling upset all morning. It occurs to me as I write this that what I am really worried about is not my dad leaving her alone at home, but his leaving her for good. And what would happen if my father was no longer around to take care of her? I don't want to have to drop everything and take over, but of course I would have to. I feel selfish for thinking this way. Guilty, too. And sad. Nicky and I are just beginning a couple's life together, and we're not ready yet to add a third: not a child, and certainly not a mother. Yet I feel certain that if my father couldn't do it, the responsibility of caring for my mother would fall to me, her only daughter. My brothers (both living in different time zones, in Washington State and Colorado) would help as much as they could, but they have built their lives far away, and in the end, I've been the one who has stayed closest to home in every way.

I've always been the homebody. When I was in college, I drove to New Jersey every few weeks to wash my clothes and sleep in my old bed. And when I had to spend my first Christmas away from my family during my junior year abroad in France, I was sick all day. When I was in college, and my parents told me they'd decided to move from New Jersey to New Hampshire, I was devastated to lose them and to lose my old hometown. I haven't always been great about calling my family—this once-a-week habit is a new one—but I was always around. My brothers were different. They were willing to move to Seattle and Boulder without making any promises to ever come home. They have started new lives and, in some ways, closed the door on their old ones.

Is this another one of those women things? Is it always the girl who ends up taking care of her parents? Not that I'm complaining: this is not a full-time job for me, the way it is for my father. Even thinking about my mother doesn't take up all of my time. It comes in waves. It was the same when my ex-boyfriend Kevin and I broke up—the feelings would be awful for a few hours, then OK for a few hours, awful for a few days, then OK for a few days, until finally I only thought about him every once in a while. That's how my feelings about Mom are, only less self-conscious and more serious: I'm fine for a while, then I'm crippled by sadness. And then—even worse—it goes away again. Sometimes, if I've had a difficult phone call from her, or if there has been news from my father that she's doing worse, I'll have a dream I don't quite remember and wake up crying. You can't hide from your mother, as we all know. And I don't want to hide from mine.

APRIL

Last night I dreamed I went to my high school reunion, and Kevin drove up to the door in his old mustard-yellow '79 Nova with the hole in the floor. He was wearing tough-guy clothes and smoking (which he never did in real life). It was straight out of a Mad Max movie.

Kevin was my boyfriend at the end of college and for a few years after that, when I first started to notice that my mother was forgetting things. This was before things got bad, before the scary car trip from New Hampshire that finally signaled something was terribly awry. Kevin and I were visiting my parents in New Hampshire. They had just moved a few months before, and Mom couldn't remember where anything was kept in the kitchen. At first I dismissed her confusion as the result of moving, but when I had mastered the drawers and cabinets by the end of the weekend and my mother was still opening every door in search of a bowl, I mentioned to Kevin that there might be something wrong. I'll never forget him telling me that his grandmother, who had severe dementia and was living in a nursing home, had started off with symptoms very much like my mother's. I was furious at him for even suggesting that my mother could have an old person's disease. My mother is only in her fifties, I told him. It couldn't possibly be that.

Six years ago, I wasn't ready to believe that there was

anything wrong with my mother at all. The dream reminds me that Kevin was right all along.

~

Of course, after six years of not hearing anything from him, Kevin called—two days after my dream. Coincidence? I think not. We talked for almost an hour. Hearing his voice was unsettling and strange. We hadn't spoken since we broke up. It had been so long that I had no idea what he was doing with his life, or even where he was living. He told me the reason he called: a few weeks ago he had been in a serious car accident, and although he wasn't hurt, he took the close call as a reminder that life is short. Afterward he started calling people he hadn't talked to in a long time, including me. He had read the article in the paper about our wedding, so he knew I was married. He was still single. His sister had had a baby. He told me he had moved out of the city as well, to a town not far away, and he asked if I'd like to get together sometime. It sounded reasonable enough to me, even nice—a casual dinner with an old friend who happened to be an ex-boyfriend—so I said OK. I chose a Wednesday, partly because Nicky would be in the city for basketball and wouldn't be left alone.

I didn't feel as nonchalant as I was pretending to be. The dinner plans seemed alternatively risqué and unthreatening, as if I were breaking a promise I never needed to make. I have this policy of not remaining friends with exes, not because I don't care about them, but simply because the idea of taking love and whittling it down to a casual friendship has always seemed impossible to me. With Kevin it was particularly difficult. He was, I suppose, my first grown-up boyfriend. After we broke up I was never able to explain clearly why it ended, although I was sure that our separation was necessary. It had something to do with knowing we weren't ready to get married, or maybe that we weren't right for each other, or both.

When I mentioned the dinner to Nicky, he seemed cheerfully uninterested in the whole thing. I was getting the impression that this was no big deal. My puny old crushes and ex-flames had been pounded and extinguished by my mighty wedding vows. Either that or my husband was just plain oblivious.

~

Went to my first pottery class last night. I was expecting to walk into a room full of earthy, artsy, vegetarian women who would teach me about moon phases and tantric breathing, but instead I joined a group of ordinary people from town, three women and two men, who had been taking the class for a few years. As I practiced wedging lumps of clay, I listened to them talk. Their chitchat was astoundingly depressing. One guy's wife had breast cancer and had been screwed over by a series of lousy doctors. A woman with two kids was complaining that she hadn't seen a movie in over a year. Another one was drinking her second tall boy of the evening as she bemoaned her husband's long hours at work. Everyone seemed damaged in one way or another, roughed up. It was so sad, these marriages fraught with problems and disappointments. I felt the same as I did in that Alzheimer's meeting: that this was the future, and it looked grim. I kept silent all evening. What was I going to say to them, that Nicky and I dance to reggae music in the kitchen as we cook dinner together and still have great sex? That there may be no shower in our house, but Nicky sits on the edge of my bath and reads to me? I was afraid they'd try to convince me that they had once been so happy—and that it doesn't last.

I did make two small clay bowls with the help of my teacher, Crystal, who, I discovered, is a vegetarian and likes to belly dance on the weekends. Thank God someone lived up to my expectations.

~

Visited Mom and Dad over the weekend. It was hard. Mom wasn't doing so well. She seemed distracted, unable to concentrate. Her usual joy at having people around was dulled somehow. Lately she seems bent on believing that we all demand that she be happy all the time, so in the middle of complaining about something, she'll suddenly cut herself off and put on this big fake smile and say, "Oh, well, I'm *fine*." I told her she should complain whenever she wants, that she's earned the right to be difficult. She laughed at me then, and told me I was right. But she won't say when something's bothering her. Or can't.

At one point during the weekend we were on a hike and along the trail came across some other hikers who were lost. They asked for directions, and as my father went over the map with one of them, my mother and I chatted with the other two. Throughout the conversation, I found myself filling in the blanks she left in her conversation, like when the other hikers asked how far we'd come, she replied, "Oh, it hasn't been bad, really—the usual," and I piped in that we'd been walking for about two miles. When they asked if we'd been up to the top of the mountain, she said, "Oh, yes," as I said, "No, it's our first time." As soon as the other hikers had left, she turned to me and sternly said that I shouldn't treat her like a baby. I didn't answer immediately because I didn't want to say the wrong thing. Finally I simply said I was sorry, that I didn't mean to be condescending. She looked at me quizzically. "I'm sorry for making you feel bad," I said. "I don't feel bad," she replied. "But you said I was treating you like a baby," I said. "No, I didn't," she said. And that was that.

The absurdity of our typical interactions is perfectly demonstrated by setting the table: Mom puts two knives at each place, glasses for plates, plates on the chairs, etc. When she leaves, I rush around the table, putting everything in its proper place. By the time I turn around, she has circled the table again, piling forks on spoons and tearing up paper napkins.

As usual I feel guilty—concerned about my father and how he's holding up (after another vain attempt to convince him to join a support group); angry with Mom for being unwell and not admitting it; unsure of how to behave around her and yet positive that I could be doing a better job of it.

I feel tired and vulnerable. I want to curl up with Nicky and hide. And why shouldn't I? I'm not exactly winning any prizes in the daughter department.

~

Last night was my dinner with Kevin. All day I was vaguely nervous. Would we pick up fighting where we left off? Would we be attracted to each other? I tried to picture what I looked like six years ago and compare it with how I looked now. Did I look older? Would he be bald? I'm not sure what I was hoping for, but I think I was looking forward to seeing another side of me—or maybe a slice of my old life—reflected in him. In the car on the way, I pulled out the directions to the restaurant that I'd jotted on the back of a receipt. "Bear right," I had written—and then I noticed underneath, in Nicky's handwriting, "Think of Nicky." After "through the flashing yellow," he had written: "Picture Nicky." After "right at first light," I read: "Remember Nicky." My unfazable husband was actually jealous—or at least he knew me well enough to know I could use a laugh about then. I realized then that it's easy enough for everyone to act casual about an ex. The trick is to really feel that way.

In the years I was together with Kevin, I was always running late. This was a problem between us. Over the past few years, I've gotten better, but for some reason that evening I was still a half-hour late getting to the restaurant. Was I regressing for the occasion? I figured he would be annoyed, but oddly he didn't seem to notice. After the awkward hug and hello, and after the initial surprise of finding ourselves face-to-face, we settled into an uneventful evening. He was still funny and charming, he had plenty of hair, and his life clearly hadn't fallen apart without me. In fact, all signs indicated that he was happier than ever: he was doing well in his job, he had a new dog, and he had fallen for a banker with dark hair. There were no dramatic revelations (the banker was, in fact, female), just the palpable, shared calm of no longer needing to work so hard at getting along.

Despite all this playing nice, however, it was no casual

dinner with a friend. When I knocked over the salt shaker, he laughingly pointed out that I had always been clumsy. "I'm not clumsy," I snapped. "I'm *chronically late*." He couldn't believe I didn't think of myself as clumsy. I couldn't believe he'd forgotten all the fights about my being on time. As the things we thought we knew about each other washed away with our talk, I realized we had become strangers, friendly strangers; and that if we wanted to know each other again, we'd have to start over in the context of our new lives.

On the whole, an undramatic event. When I arrived home, Nicky had just gotten back from basketball and seemed only casually interested—perhaps not wanting to place any more importance on the dinner than it deserved, or perhaps having already expressed all his anxieties in his editorial notes on my directions. Marriage and age conspire to flatten out a life. This is a good thing, but it's also a boring thing. Everything is pleasantly rounded, but I feel like nothing is on the edge anymore.

~

Have been going to the gym twice a week, which feels good even if it doesn't seem to be changing much about my body.

Nicky has had two rejections on his novel, and the air in our little house is filled with gloom and doom. We're both really worried about money. I sent out a bunch of résumés to local colleges to try to get some kind of teaching job to supplement our income. Nicky—glumly—is doing the same.

~

Barely made it through today—I was in a terrible, terrible mood, bad enough that everything I wrote looked crappy to me, and every item of clothing I put on made me look ugly. I quit working early and went to an afternoon movie (a dumb flick, though that didn't stop me from sobbing through the whole thing), then came home and watched about four hours of TV until I acquired the brain-dead glaze of lifeless consumers across America.

When I get into a state like this, Nicky will sometimes try to cheer me up, as he did tonight. He wants to help fix it, somehow; but of course I'm in a mood that cannot be defined, let alone repaired. I think he thinks it's a reflection on him, or on his ability to be a good husband, if I'm not happy. Nicky wants to take action, to plow ahead, to make things better and get on with it. I want to let my feelings run their course, to experience them uninterrupted, and then let them dissipate on their own. I finally told him that sometimes I need to be left alone in my bad moods. Why is it so hard for me to tell him that? Is it because I think he'll stop trying to help if I push him away?

In some ways we're acting more like each other, and I suppose that should be refreshing. I'm guilty of the same dumb silences and gruff answers as my husband used to be. He's acting emotionally erratic and professionally insecure in the way I thought I trademarked early on. Am I glooming and dooming in order to generously distract him from his recent funk—or to selfishly restake my claim as the vulnerable and unstable one between us? Could he be sulking in order to distract *me* from my sadness about my mother—or because he's tired of protecting me from all my anxieties while I skip off to flirty dates with ex-boyfriends that he can't even bring himself to ask about? Just when I think we're firmly rooted in our roles, we switch places. And just when I think we're infinitely flexible— freed from those silly clichés that other husbands and wives fall into—we're not. The hard part of marriage, recently, has not been having to get used to the other person's inflexible behavior and deep-set personality; it's been getting used to the fact that we're always changing. We are always responding to each other: a hundred times a day, a hundred ways a minute. That's what makes me so attached to my husband. And that's what makes me, at times like this, so enormously tired.

~

On mornings after days like yesterday, I awake and tiptoe around, hoping the feeling from the day before will stay away. But today there were flowers popping up all over the garden, and the cloud had definitely passed. I had a good but groggy conversation with Nicky in the early morning about my seeing Kevin: turns out he was curious after all—but more about my memories and opinion of the relationship than about the guy or the dinner. Now I'm sitting in bed writing with Nicky asleep next to me and Emma snoring in the corner of the room. My family.

MAY

I have an interview for a teaching job next week. It sounds perfect: two days a week teaching college writing to freshmen. (It's always amazing when sending out résumés actually results in something.) I spent the day trying to come up with sample lesson plans for the semester. I wish I had kept all my old college papers.

~

Had dinner with Natalie last night, just the two of us. I never had spent time alone with her before, mostly because she was Nicky's friend first of all, and I saw her only when Nicky and I went out with her and her husband, Paul. Before now, if anyone from the foursome were to go out alone, it would be Natalie and Nicky or Paul and Nicky. I've always held the prime position as the outsider, the observer, and I was vaguely reluctant to give that up and become pals with Natalie. As usual, it was the other person who did the right thing and made the gesture of friendship, and as it turned out we had a good time. That's why I like Natalie. Without people like her, I would sit at home and think about how mysterious I am.

The only bad thing about writing, other than running out of things to say, is that the pay—like the prose—comes in little spurts, and when it does come, it's never enough. We're lucky not to have a mortgage or huge debts, but still, money is never far from our minds. Things are going to be better this fall when I start teaching, anyway. They'd be even better if Nicky could sell his novel to some eager publisher who has yet to materialize. Then again, I suppose if we had a ton of money I'd feel like we had to *do* something about it: buy a house or have a baby or go live in Italy. Maybe it's more relaxing—in a stressful sort of way—to be a little broke. At least I'm doing what I want with my life. At least I'm doing what I want with my life. At least I'm doing what I want with my life. Is this working yet?

~

The warm weather makes me think of weddings. I still go over ours in my mind, trying to see it from an onlooker's perspective, but of course I can't. It still churns up a self-conscious excitement when I think of it. On the other hand, being married is starting to feel completely natural. I don't even notice when I refer to Nicky as my husband.

We seem to have settled into each other, and in each other's company we can be alone or together without realizing we're making adjustments. And our days have settled into a pleasant routine.

In the mornings I come downstairs at eight, two hours after Nicky. He has already done his sit-ups and made coffee. I walk to the mailbox to pick up the newspaper, and I sit in his office to read while he works. Then I usually make something for breakfast, oatmeal or eggs or toast. Nicky comes into the kitchen and we eat together. On the days that Nicky works at home, we go into our separate offices and work until lunch. When all of this comes together, it's a really nice life. There's nothing I like more than working in my office and having Nicky buzz me on the intercom and ask me bizarre questions, like how to spell "cardamom." (That's right, by the way—I checked.) I love how much we know about each other, that he's stopped offering me orange juice but knows that I'll sometimes eat an orange. And yet there are still surprises, like when he announced he was going on a no-pie diet in an attempt to eat more healthfully—his theory being that he should eliminate only one beloved sweet at a time. (Since then he's managed to compensate for the lack of pie with ice cream bars, chocolate cake, and candy corn, so I'm sure he's not starving.)

On weekend mornings, we make love, stay in bed drinking coffee out of the mugs I made in my pottery class, read the paper, and then stumble downstairs at eleven, starving for breakfast. I have to admit our life together is good, despite how neurotic I am most of the time.

~

The *Self* columns have been well received so far, according to my editor at the magazine, which is thrilling. I meet strangers and old friends who assure me that they read my column regularly while standing in the supermarket line or waiting for the dentist. A few weeks ago, a book editor called and asked if I had thought about turning my columns into a book. She described what she had in mind, an honest look at what planning a wedding and getting married is all about. I've been trying to get a proposal together to send to my agent. It's an exciting idea, but I'm trying not to get my hopes up.

Just as this good news came in for me, Nicky's has been the opposite. His agent sent out his novel to a few publishers, and it has been received with deafening silence. Nicky is intense, distracted, and for the first time I've ever seen, unable to work. He clearly sees this as a failure and therefore sees failure in everything he does. To top it off, he was rejected for a local job as a library assistant. And to top that off, a long magazine piece he'd just finished was rejected by his editor's boss. I have a pit in my stomach to see him kicked around like this. I wish it were me instead. Well, no I don't. But I sort of wish I wished it were me.

I keep telling him that things can't get any worse and

then they do. I thought that being married, and having me to help, would make his disappointments easier, but at times like this I think it makes them seem more serious—a threat to his ability to provide, to be a good husband. These are the ups and downs of our first year together, and they're more terrifying because we don't have any prece-dent to look back on: we haven't watched ourselves get through this before. I *know* that Nicky is going to pull through, sell a novel, be successful. The catch is that he doesn't always believe it himself. When we first met I was always afraid of future changes, fearful that what we were signing up for might change for the worse. But I guess now that we're seeing some real-life bad times, I realize that they're not so bad.

It's strange that *I'm* doing fine, for once: I have the magazine column to work on this summer, I landed a great teaching job for the fall, and, if a miracle happens, I might even have a book deal, too. So if I have to, I can carry us for a while. I always knew the two of us could survive any storm together, but frankly I'm surprised to discover that I'm the one putting a steady arm around my husband, and not the other way around. He seems surprised, too.

~

On Saturday night, my husband took the train into the city for a friend's bachelor party, where—I found out later—the guys made toasts over a steak dinner and then, for dessert, watched an "exotic dancer" slink around the room in nothing but the groom's tie. I had expected that this would be on the agenda, and although I knew that Nicky wasn't going to the party because there would be a stripper—his own choice for a bachelor party had been to play basketball with a bunch of friends and then go out for beers—it still made me feel uncomfortable that he was going *despite* it. It wasn't the girl so much as the scenario: me at home in the country, with the dog asleep at the foot of the bed, and him in the private room of a steakhouse in the city with a bunch of guys and one naked girl.

That night I was expecting him to catch the train that would bring him home at 1:30 A.M., but as it turned out he arrived at two-thirty instead. I was furious, and although I told him it was because he woke me up when he stumbled in, the real reason was, of course, the stripper. I'm not sure I felt jealous or threatened, exactly. It was more that I felt stupid, the little lady waiting for her man. I probably should have made plans to go out with some friends instead of sitting home and stewing, but those plans would have just been a reaction to Nicky's evening out, and I was trying as hard as I could not to react at all.

I was still mad the next morning as we sat outside and read the Sunday paper. I knew that if I told Nicky I wanted him to skip any future bachelor parties that might include a dancer or late-night topless bar, he would agree simply because I asked. But that wasn't what I wanted, exactly. I wanted an explanation. What was the point?

When I asked him, Nicky shrugged and couldn't help me. He didn't seem to know.

~

Lately when I drive down Main Street, I notice all the high school girls walking home. They're all tiny with tan, long legs. Up close you can see that they're teenagers, but from a distance they look like beautiful women. It makes me feel old, realizing that these kids weren't even born when I was starting high school.

I think this goes back to the other night, which made me feel, despite how ridiculous I know it is to feel it, that in watching this woman "perform," Nicky was somehow relegating me—the wife at home—to the vast pool of ordinary women in the world, the kind of women you might marry and have a life with, but not the ones you're eager to see undressed. In my mind, these ogling men became equally pathetic—kind, hardworking husbands turned into nerdy, suit-wearing lechers who needed some kind of thrill injected into their otherwise unfulfilling lives. I didn't want to fall into the former category any more than I wanted Nicky to fit the latter.

In the end, in order to restore some normalcy in the house, Nicky told me that he wouldn't go to any more of the damned things. Not, he insisted, because I didn't want him to, but because he didn't care about them anyway. But I know it was because of me. Which is marriage, it seems.

We compromise when we can, when it makes life easier. In doing so we reveal our true selves to each other—slowly and deliberately, the way a dancer teases a crowd—until there's nothing left but our naked selves.

~

Ah, the joy of life in the country: mouse turds on the stove every morning, spiders all over the place, and an acute awareness of growing older as a result of watching, up close, a new spring. The forsythia bush in the yard is blooming already, and a spray of crocuses across the lawn have already come and gone.

I've been sick all week, with a fever and sneezing and coughing. I suspect it's a result of my allergies, which are so much worse here than they are in the city. Sleeping felt like work—as if I had a few dozen little tasks to accomplish each hour.

Now it's 10:30 A.M., and I'm sitting on my front stoop recuperating. Emma is lying under my legs and sniffing at a bug that just crawled into a crack between the bricks.

I've been reading a biography of Zelda Fitzgerald. Zelda had already been married, published a book, had a kid, traveled all over, and gone crazy by the time she turned thirty. By then she was past her prime. I haven't done any of those things yet. I haven't even gone properly insane. Even worse, I feel as if I'm not being properly eccentric these days; I'm not sure whether it's being married that is making me feel so ordinary, or whether it's that we're no longer in the city among all the weirdos and freaks. I miss being one of them, even when my weirdness consisted only of bleaching my hair bright white or wearing platform sneakers. Nicky has a tattoo on his shoulder, but out here he's kept it primly covered up by his flannel shirts. I have a lime-green pleather jacket and leopard-skin tights that I used to sport in the East Village, but since moving they've remained stowed away in the closet. The married Amanda doesn't wear pleather. The married Amanda doesn't even live in New York City. Then again, I tell myself, the married Amanda has the confidence to do whatever she wants. And sometimes I think she will.

∼

Went to Hannah and Patrick's wedding over the weekend. What a different experience it is to be a wedding guest once you're married! I didn't have the running commentary in my mind, asking if that dress would look good on me, or if I would have preferred chocolate to vanilla cake, or whether I wanted a chowder bar. Our wedding feels like a long time ago. It makes me realize how glad I am not to have to go through being a bride again. There's this agitated excitement that radiates from the bride and groom, a frantic happiness—and an inability to concentrate on anything for more than a second or two. They really become transformed, at least for a few hours. It's no wonder brides look beautiful at their weddings, with all the adrenaline going through them. I'll bet that fifteen minutes before our wedding, Nicky and I could've lifted a car and spun it around without feeling a thing.

I'm also really happy to be married. It's starting to feel like part of my life. And sometimes like the best part.

JUNE

I finally finished a proposal and sent it to my agent last week, and today I received a formal offer of a book deal. I'm going to write a book! It's so exciting, and I can't wait to start. Of course instead of writing, I've spent the day practicing what I'm going to say on *Oprah* when whatever it is that I'm not writing becomes a smash hit.

Rather than being jealous, Nicky is thrilled and relieved that one of us is dragging our double-freelance life along. I'm relieved too. If they put my name on the contract, and even print it on the book, that means I'm actually an author. I daydream of sending a copy to the jerks at the old law firm, but that would probably mean that some poor girl like me would have totype a thank-you note, or transcribe it into legalese, or take the thing and shred it.

~

Last night was our final pottery class. Everyone brought snacks and drinks, and I expected a quiet pot luck party, but instead we all got smashed. These people have turned out to be a lot more fun than I expected. Mike made margaritas, someone else put on some crazy belly dancing music, and we all started to boogie. I danced with Crystal, then Mike, then Margot, and then I got up on a stool and danced alone. I finally dragged myself home after midnight, whereas I'm usually home by ten. I had called Nicky to tell him I was going to be late, but he waited up anyway to make sure I got back safely. It was nice that he worried.

~

A long stretch of quiet summer ahead. Nicky has decided to stop rewriting his novel and start a new one, and he got a job for the fall teaching kids at a learning center. I'm glad to see him back to his usual routine, and he seems to have made it through the spring with his humor intact. I have resurrected my one-act play and am working on it when I'm not doing magazine stuff or planning out the book.

Paul and Natalie and their families sent us a gas grill for a wedding present, so we've been cooking out every evening. It's so beautiful out here now, with the lilac trees in bloom and a sea of peonies in pink and white in the corner of the garden. We grill vegetables and shrimp kabobs, or steak for him and a veggie burger for me. We grill bananas for dessert and cover them with nuts and melted honey. We take long walks and feed carrots to the horses. We write and read and talk about writing. It's heaven. Or at least a pretty good version of earth.

~

The first question out of everyone's mouth these days seems to be "When are you going to have a baby?" It comes from our new neighbors, who make a pointed effort to praise the local school system; from my mother, who vaguely mentions how nice it will be when we bring "a bigger group" to visit for the weekend; and even from the gynecologist, who at my latest checkup gave me a twenty-minute sales pitch on the "birthing cottage" at our local hospital. (I was practically signed up for a Le Leche meeting before I was out of my paper robe.) It's unrelenting: my friend Alex, who was in the middle of researching a newspaper article on the subject, mentioned to me yesterday that the best way for me to avoid ovarian cancer is to have a baby before I turn thirty. Too late. But there's a chorus of mommies in the back of my mind, as well as a long shelf of pregnancy books in the doctor's waiting room, reminding me that if I get moving soon, I'll at least avoid the risks that come with getting pregnant after the age of thirty-five.

It's not that I mind thinking about starting a family. I'm pretty sure I want to have kids one of these days. But I miss the time when it was all hypothetical: back in college and for a few years after that, conversations with girlfriends about pregnancy focused on avoiding it at all costs. After all, we weren't dating guys we expected to marry. We were young, we were thin, and we expected to stay that way. We had big plans for our careers. Now all of my talks with friends about pregnancy have abruptly turned from con to pro.

My body, too, has joined the sabotage. It seems outrageous: what did I need with the ability to bear children between the ages of thirteen and twenty-five? What did my hormones ever do for me except to make me look dangerously like a woman on the outside when I was still a child on the inside? The irony is that now that I'm finally mature enough to bring a human into the world, I am made to feel that I'm already *too* mature—behind schedule, dragging my feet—by the subtle and not-so-subtle messages I receive every day.

Nonetheless, at times I am hit by the urge to drop everything and get pregnant. Like the afternoon I got to hold Tommy, our neighbor's adorable, well-behaved newborn. Or the evening our pregnant friend Melissa cooked us dinner, looking impossibly beautiful, a combination of happy and sexy. Or anytime I see a miniature jeans jacket in Baby Gap. But then I force myself to be rational—and find myself unable to come up with a reason that the next pregnant shopper should be me. Or, for that matter, shouldn't be.

Nicky has been treating the issue intellectually. Why would we want to bring a kid into the world now, he asks, at a point when we could barely afford the mashed carrots? He's been scouring the classified ads for a decent used car; why extend our worries to include strollers and tricycles? We are united in our hesitancy, and cornered by a world that frowns on childless couples. Two people can't be happy and healthy and in love and *not* have kids, says society. It's selfish. It's odd. It's barren. But to me, it's the reasons to *have* a child that have always seemed selfish. Sure, it would be great to see Nicky as a father. What a relief it would be to do something that would eclipse some of my anxiety about my career. How great to get to experience a new whole kind of love. Me, me, me.

Despite this, I've been thinking about babies a lot. I've even started making lists of names and trying them out on Nicky. "What about India?" I ask. "Reminds me of India Ink," he replies. "What about Charlotte?" "Too *Charlotte's Web*." "How about Daniel?" "I hated a Daniel in high school." "Jack?" "Kids will call him 'Jack and the Weinstock.'"

It's kind of fun to talk about it in a head-butting-against-a-wall kind of way, but I don't think either of us is really ready yet. So we'll wait. We've still got time. No time. Plenty of time.

~

Mom and Dad came for the weekend. It was calm and easy all weekend long, maybe because we were all on my turf. Nicky and I took them on a hike, cooked them dinner, rented a movie, kept things moving. I'm constantly aware of wanting to be with my mother and then wanting her to go away, swinging back and forth in my mind until she leaves and I breathe a sigh of relief and then immediately start thinking about when I'll see her next.

I'm getting better at this, I think; I've learned to watch Dad and see how he deals with Mom. He does everything right: he doesn't try to control her, or monitor her every move, but at the same time he knows where she is and what she's doing at every minute. It must be exhausting for him, especially when they travel, but he rarely complains. They seem to be traveling all the time now: they're even planning to go to Africa next summer. I get the feeling that Dad is trying to plan all the adventuring they can while Mom—or both of them, for that matter—are still well enough to do it.

Mom needed a haircut, so I took her to my local place.

Marta did a good job, but on the way home Mom confessed that she preferred the salon near our apartment in the city where we went last year. The guy who cut her hair there was Japanese and didn't speak any English—but I guess they had some kind of connection. You never know what's going to stick in her mind. Next time she visits I'm going to take her to the Japanese guy in the city. While we ladies were at the beauty parlor, Nicky took Dad for a tour of the firehouse, showing him twelve-foot ladders and a hydraulic windshield saw. Dad was thrilled. So was I.

JULY

Things here are quiet and lazy; it feels like a summer vacation when I was a kid, only without the vacation. For a lark, Nicky and I have been working on a screenplay. Once a week we drive to the local luncheonette and work out details of the plot. We both know that it's got about as much potential to make us money as a lottery ticket. The best thing about it is the time we spend together working on it, and sharing a daydream about our future. I'm finally feeling settled out here in the country, and my complaints about being left alone and isolated feel far away.

I'm planning a vacation to Seattle to visit Sabina, my sister-in-law, while Tony is in the North Pole on a job doing research from an icebreaker ship. He's an atmospheric scientist. If Nicky and I have children, with our luck, they'll probably get that Beesley science gene and we won't be able to understand anything they say. But I'm not thinking about kids right now. Not at all.

~

I am pleased to report that Nicky had a proper birthday this year. I gave him a beat-up first edition of *The Great Gatsby*, one of his favorite books, and we had a lovely dinner in the city with friends. I think I made up for last year (and, with any luck, raised the bar for my birthday in September).

Leaving in a week or so for Seattle: the first trip without Nicky since we got married. I'm not sure whether I've planned this simply because I want to or if some part of me is determined to prove that I can go away without my husband. In any case, I'm looking forward to it. Sabina's going to be working the whole time so I will write while she's at work and then we'll do things together in the evenings.

Mailed off my one-act play to a festival being held at our local theater, having tried and failed everywhere else. I'm so determined to see this *go* somewhere; it's a side of my writing—of my personality—that I don't want to leave behind, the experimental, magical, improvisational side of writing that only exists when you make stuff up.

AUGUST

(Seattle)

The first thing my sister-in-law told me when I got here is that she is two months pregnant. I'm going to be an aunt. Sabina isn't sick in the mornings, and she doesn't look as though she's gained weight so far. We went for a hike yesterday and she outwalked me, as usual. I went with her to a midwife appointment, which was fascinating. It made me realize how important it is to be in good shape before you get pregnant. It's like a spa here: barely any alcohol, lots of exercise, food groups abundantly represented in low-fat proportions.

When we met, Sabina and I fell for each other right away. It's like we've known each other forever. There's something about being with her, especially now that she's pregnant, that makes her seem like she's from another world. She's pretty, funny, clear-eyed, and unsentimental, and when I'm around her I find myself making lists to myself of what I should do when I get home to make myself better: start jogging, learn to meditate, quit all occasional cigarette smoking, eat more healthily. Her being pregnant makes me want to be pregnant, too. Yikes. I've come all this way to escape thinking about it, only to come face-to-face. Double yikes.

So here I am on a beautiful afternoon in Seattle, having finished my writing for the day, and instead of enjoying myself, I'm thinking of what I'm going to do when I get home to make my life better, whether it be to have kids or to do sit-ups regularly. This, I think, is my biggest problem: I'm like Ms. Pac-Man, chomping along, eating everything in sight, instead of taking a minute to savor what I've got. I have to remember that Sabina's life is her own and has nothing to do with the progression of mine—that she and my brother chose to start a family for their own reasons, at their own pace. This isn't a competition, it's a major life choice; and so I can only look to Nicky and to myself— and not into the windows of Baby Gap—for guidance.

~

(Back at Home)

It has been fairly quiet for the past few weeks. I'm on my second-to-last column and starting to think about how to write this book, which I'm supposed to have started already. I'm going to include my mother in the book, which is alternatively terrifying and liberating. I know that good things can come of it if I can write honestly about my feelings; I just want to be sure I do a good job. I never wrote a word about her in the magazine columns, partly because I wasn't ready, and partly because I couldn't have explained in a nine-hundred-word article that my mother had dementia and that I was heartbroken. I just couldn't.

~

This morning Nicky and I went to our local church; it was the first time we'd been in front of a minister since we've been married, and I actually made it through the whole service without crying. I prayed for my mother and for my family, and for once I felt calm instead of grief-stricken. And when it was over and the congregation spilled out in front of the church, I suddenly realized that Nicky and I knew a lot of the people there. We saw our neighbors from down the road, and Dorothy and Dan, whom Nicky met through the fire department, and a couple we met in New York who spend the weekends out here, and Mike from my pottery class. It actually felt as if we were part of the town. I need to think this way, to develop a new positive attitude.

But what struck me most of all was something the pastor said. He told a story about being at a farm in Iowa in March. In the middle of an icy field was a huge cylinder made of wire that was once used for storing corn. A corncrib, I think he said. The rest of the field had been plowed and was at the time a lonely expanse of frozen dirt. The only sign of life was an oak tree which had grown up inside the corncrib and flourished there. It had been protected from the plow, over the years, by this outdated and now-unused piece of farm equipment.

Although he was trying to make a point about religion, the story seemed to sum up what this funny and old-fashioned institution of marriage is all about. By creating a life within the restrictions of our partnership, we will grow stronger and freer than either of us would have been able to on our own. I think the metaphor also applies to this town: we've been restricted in some ways, by the lack of socializing and sushi, of stand-up showers and all-night diners, but in return we've had the calm and the time to get better as writers, and as a couple.

~

Things that stink about living in the country despite my new positive attitude:

1. grocery stores close at 5:59
2. no take-out for ten miles
3. no occasions to wear cool shoes
4. dinner is over by six and we are then doomed to a night of bad TV
5. splinters
6. snakes
7. fear of Lyme disease

~

Found out that my play was accepted in the local one-act festival. It's going up in October. I feel like I've won a Tony Award. What a great town.

~

I just got a call from Sabina. She had a miscarriage. I feel awful for her. She sounded sad, and I think her confidence is shaken. Why isn't this easy? When you finally decide you want to have a baby, you're ready to take on that awesome responsibility, it doesn't seem fair that it should be difficult even to get started. It scares me to think how tenuous parenthood can be, even if you've got everything to give to a new baby and are willing to put your life on hold to do so.

She says they're going to wait a couple months and start again. I was so upset that she ended up comforting me, explaining that this is nature's way of weeding out the babies that wouldn't survive through the whole pregnancy.

I realize that I was treating the idea of having a baby as a "step," a next logical stage, without thinking about the actual experience of being pregnant—let alone the risks involved.

~

After almost a year of marriage, there are still moments when I wake up in the morning, see my husband sleeping next to me, and think, Where did this guy come from, and how did he get in my bed? After a moment of panic, I tell myself that the bed is *our* bed, that he is *my* husband, and that we have made a public and private pact to spend the rest of our lives together. This happens so quickly that you'd never know I missed a beat. But in the midst of these little lapses, as I inspect his face mashed into the pillow, with that dumb, sweet, vulnerable look around his mouth, I can't quite remember where—and for that matter why—I picked this guy up. It's then that I realize what Billy Joel was singing about in the early eighties when I was still sporting a jean jacket and frosty blue eye shadow: The Stranger hits me right between the eyes.

You never really know anyone, I suppose, even the person you're married to. And this is probably a good thing. There is plenty about Nicky that I don't need to know, like if he thinks I've gained a little weight, or if he's had a sexy dream about one of my friends. I certainly do not want to know what it is about me that might make Nicky wonder, from time to time, exactly why he got married and how he ended up marrying me. I figure it's better to be left in the dark about some things. If I am ever spooked by the amount of mystery in our relationship, I can always fall back on the things that, after nearly twelve months of better and worse, richer and poorer, and sickness and health, I am able to predict with total accuracy. Like that Nicky will never fully grasp the intricacies of my clothes-washing system. Or that whenever he tries to be a chivalrous hubby by holding his umbrella over my head, I will always end up either soaked or poked. And I can

217

predict with confidence that we will be arguing about his eyesight well into our eighties: he will insist his vision is perfectly fine, and I will nag him to wear his glasses.

Knowing a lot about Nicky's habits and knowing a little about his soul is good enough for me. It's what I'd like him to have of me as well. And it makes me want to learn more.

SEPTEMBER

I've been in back-to-school mode, fixing up my office and building bookshelves, buying a grade book and some pens, reading textbooks for teaching ideas. It makes me realize that I never actually *built* anything when I lived in the city. I had no office to decorate, no job that required my preparation. And it never seemed as if there was time to read.

This time last year, Nicky and I were feverishly, almost hysterically counting the hours until our wedding. It seems like a million years ago. Tomorrow is our first anniversary. I'm trying to decide whether this first year has been as difficult as everyone said. In the end, I guess the answer is yes and no. There have been tough times, especially in the winter, with our getting used to the move, and my feeling lonely, and our trying to nudge our careers into flight. But summer has been lovely. Now that the fall is coming again, I feel more prepared, as if I know better what to expect. Even if I don't.

As for my mother, she gets worse in tiny steps, just as we as a family get better at figuring out how to make her as comfortable and as happy as possible. I think we also get better, in those same tiny steps, at accepting her illness and making the best of it. There have been times this year when I've felt more alive than ever before, and I know it's because my mother has reminded me that what really matters in the end, when everything else is stripped away, is love and companionship—a good laugh in the kitchen, a walk in the woods—which when added together make a marriage.

~

For our anniversary, we went for a picnic in Storm King park, where we took tentative bites of year-old wedding cake (Nicky's mom had frozen the top for us) in the shadows of giant outdoor sculptures by artists like Mark Di Suvero and Richard Serra. I gave Nicky an old lithograph which showed a mountain near our house that we'd once climbed together. He gave me an electric typewriter, an IBM Selectric (the last of its breed), that I'd been coveting for a long time. We finished our lunch, took a long walk, and drove home as the sun went down. At home there were messages on our answering machine from my parents and from Nicky's, from Sonya and Julia and Elliot, all saying congratulations. All day I felt lucky.

Oh yeah, I dreamed last night I was pregnant, and I knew it was going to be twins. Sounds like double luck to me—whatever these babies, and their parents, turn out to be.

Afterward

And so ended the first year of our marriage. My one-act play was performed five times over two weekends at the tiny local theater by the train station, with a few dozen of our neighbors in attendance, and I felt prouder of it than anything I've ever done. Sabina is now halfway through a healthy pregnancy, and Nicky is halfway through a healthy new novel. One recent afternoon, Nicky and I decided to move back to New York City. We missed our friends too much, all the action and the weirdos and the diversity. It happened like this: Nicky was on the phone, and he was talking about how nice it was being in the country, and how much writing we were getting done, and how easy it is to get a doctor's appointment. As I listened from the couch, I realized that there was an unspoken "but" at the end of his sentence, the kind of looming "but" that comes toward the end of a wonderful vacation: *It's all really nice, but we want to come home now*. It's been a terrific retreat. But even the best retreats have to come to an end.

We began to talk about finding an apartment, and that discussion led to an excited analysis of the number of bedrooms we wanted, which in turn led to the question of a baby to put in one of the bedrooms. And it was Nicky who said out loud that he wanted to have a baby soon. I loved that he said it first, that for once I wasn't the one pushing us on to the next step. I'm excited for the experience, despite knowing how much we'll miss our lazy weekends at home and our quiet evenings of red wine and grilled dinner.

Emma is in good shape, although she sulks at the suggestion of returning to a land of concrete and gutters when she now has the luxury of grass, mud, and horse dung to roll in. I still procrastinate and get less work done than I'd like. Nicky still does his sit-ups every morning, then writes from 6:30 A.M. until 1:00 P.M., then has lunch, then does a little more work, just for laughs, in the afternoon.

Since that crazy day last September when we publicly made ourselves an official couple, we've had plenty of time to get used to married life, and these days I really like it. When Nicky and I were dating, I was a newly arrived Dorothy in Oz: I had everything I needed the whole time, but I didn't know it. Now that Nicky is permanently a part of my life, I've got courage, brains, love, and a home that I never knew I had. And if I mentioned that I wanted ruby slippers, he'd probably surprise me with them the next day, hidden in a manuscript box. I feel calmer and more confident. I'm surprised by how willing I am to work as a team, to learn from Nicky how to help him, and to teach him new and subtler ways of helping me. I'm not talking about the kind of help that leads to perfectly washed socks or keeping me dry in the rain, but help with the big stuff: our families, our careers, our relationship, our future. I've never been good at asking for this kind of help, and Nicky hasn't either. But this year we've had to learn how to lean on each other, how to share responsibility for things we always assumed would be our own problems—individual and unshared, macho and girly. Those distinctions are gone now that we're married. We don't share every little burden, but when it comes to something important, we know to join our strength and bear the weight together.

Our lives have changed dramatically in the past two years. We've moved from the city to the country, apartment to house, neighborhood to dirt road, and—someday soon—back again. We've started new careers and new projects in those careers, and we've both stumbled into goofy hobbies. If you had asked me before I met Nicky whether I could picture myself spending a year in a ramshackle old house taking pottery classes and practicing yoga, I'd have laughed so hard my sunglasses would have fallen into my cappuccino. If you had told me that my future husband would be a former editor turned log splitter and firefighter, and that we'd both be writers, I'd have dropped my Barneys shopping bag into a puddle.

It should come as no surprise that our new life sometimes feels like a shooting star—a flash of something unfamiliar and fleeting, as beautiful and odd as the lunar eclipse we saw on our honeymoon a year ago. Even though I may think I can predict what's going to happen next between Nicky and me, the significance of my predictions shrinks in the face of the giant uncertainties and monster thrills that surely await us.

~

As for my family, I think I'm getting the hang of being a wife and a daughter at the same time, and have already learned that I'll never be an expert at either. I've begun to think and dream about my mother in a new way, still loving her so much that sometimes it hurts, but doing it without drowning in sadness. I am slowly learning how to care for her—and care about her—without letting go of myself, how to be attentive without being obsessive, and, most of all, how not to strain my eyes for a glimpse around a bend or over a hill, but to concentrate on rounding and climbing with pleasure. After all, it's she who taught me to hike in the first place.

My mother probably won't read this book—she doesn't read anymore—but she will be happy that I'm happy to have written one, which is even better. When I first heard her diagnosis, I imagined that she was dying; but I know that she's living every day, and living well. She and my father go on long hikes several times a week, and when they're not hiking, they're traveling. I go up to New Hampshire to see them every month, or they come to us. At times I forget that there are things about my mother's past that I will never learn about, and pieces of her personality that I will never know again. But as she is, my mother loves me, with all the immediacy and intensity she has now. And for my part, I love her more than ever, with everything I have. And what I have is increasing all the time.

When my parents came to visit me the last time, I saw them in a new light, not as victims of some doctor's note, but rather as an example to follow: fighters who have never lost hope of victory. My mother relaxes in my father's presence, accepts his help and his gentle solicitousness. Dad takes care of Mom, watches her, listens to what she says and answers her with all the respect in the world. Thirty-three years, so far, of love and work and marching on. The power of marriage is in its endurance, its self-sufficiency, and its willingness to accept change. I can only wish as much for myself.

And I do. Every day.